Uncle John's
BATHROOM READER®
DOG LOVER'S
COMPANION

Uncle John's BATHROOM READER®

DOG L**·**VER'S COMPANION

PORTABLE PRESS

Bathroom Readers' Institute
San Diego, California, and Ashland, Oregon

Some of the stories included in this edition have been reprinted or
excerpted from the following Bathroom Reader titles: *Uncle John's
Ahh-Inspiring Bathroom Reader, Uncle John's All-Purpose Extra Strength
Bathroom Reader, Uncle John's Bathroom Reader Plunges Into History
Again, Uncle John's Giant 10th Anniversary Bathroom Reader, Uncle
John's Great Big Bathroom Reader, Uncle John's Legendary Lost
Bathroom Reader,* and *Uncle John's Unstoppable Bathroom Reader.*

"Bathroom Reader," "Portable Press," and "Bathroom Readers'
Institute" are registered trademarks of Baker & Taylor, Inc.
All rights reserved.

For information, write The Bathroom Readers' Institute
Portable Press, 10350 Barnes Canyon Road, San Diego, CA 92121
e-mail: unclejohn@btol.com

ISBN 13: 978-1-59223-823-1 ISBN 10: 1-59223-823-8

Library of Congress Cataloging-in-Publication Data

Uncle John's bathroom reader dog lover's companion.
p. cm.
ISBN 978-1-59223-823-1 (hardcover)
1. Dogs--Miscellanea. 2. Dogs--Humor. I. Title: Bathroom reader
dog lover's companion. II. Title: Dog lover's companion.
SF426.2.U53 2007
636.7--dc22

2007021788

Printed in Canada
07 08 09 10 11   10 9 8 7 6 5 4 3 2 1

Contents

Doggone Great Animation

For Fun

Good (and Bad) Eats

History

Inspirational Tails

Just the Facts

Mixed Bag

Thank You!

The Bathroom Readers' Institute sincerely thanks the following
people (and dogs) whose advice and support made this book possible.

Gordon Javna

JoAnn Padgett

Melinda Allman

Amy Miller

Julia Papps

Michael Brunsfeld

Sydney Stanley

Michelle Sedgwick

Monica Maestas

Richard Willis

Angela Kern

Mana Monzavi

Laurel Graziano

Dylan Drake

Cynthia Francisco

Stephanie Spadaccini

Friesens

Bea, Bruno, Porter, and Bubbles

BRI Scholars

We also want to thank the talented writers
who contributed selections to this work.

Tobias Buckell

Myles Callum

J. Carroll

Jenness I. Crawford

Beth Fhaner

Katie Jones

Vickey Kalambakal

Kerry Kern

Megan Kern

Toney Lee

Dan Mansfield

Elizabeth McNulty

Lisa Meyers

Debbie Pawlak

Jennifer Payne

Sue Steiner

Diana Moes VandeHoef

Bonnie VandeWater

Dog Lovers Unite!

Last August, right around National Dog Day, while we were out buying soy ice cream doggy treats in celebration, we got to thinking: Why not do a book about dogs? Sure, there are countless training and behavior manuals out there, but where were the stories—the heroic mutts who save the day . . . the underdogs who pull out wins at Westminster and the World's Ugliest Dog contest . . . the K-9 units that braved World War I's front lines to get the soldiers their smokes? Dogs are man's best friend for a reason, and it's not just because they sit and stay.

So, to honor our favorite pets (and the humans who love them), we filled this book with some of our favorite dog stories, facts, and trivia. Read about . . .

- The backstage secrets of Underdog, Scooby Doo, and Rin Tin Tin.
- Inspirational tales about the world's smallest police dog, an amputee pooch from Turkey, and a Rottweiler who saved a little girl during the 1989 San Francisco earthquake.
- Talented canines who paint, surf, and skateboard.

And because we're in the business of digging up dog-gone fascinating information, we also asked questions . . .

- How did pit bulls get such a bad reputation?
- Why does my pooch circle three times before he lies down?
- What dogs brought fame to the Iditarod trail?
- What four-legged friends inspired Picasso, Toulouse-Lautrec, and Warhol?
- Can I register my dog with the American Kennel Club?
- What legendary werewolf inspired a Harry Potter character?
- Could my home really be powered by dog poop?
- Who invented dry dog food? Milk-Bones? Flea collars?

From poodles to puggles, Labs to Lhasa Apsos, salukis to Saint Bernards, they're all here. So take a seat, grab a chew toy, and settle in. *Uncle John's Bathroom Reader Dog Lover's Companion* is for you.

As always, go with the flow.

—Uncle John and the BRI Staff

The First
"Last Great Race"

*Only the best and the bravest can run the
Iditarod—which makes it a fitting tribute to the heroic
men and dogs who helped save an Alaskan town.*

To Nome!

Imagine a two- to three-week race with the world's greatest runners moving at high speed for more than 1,150 miles. Instead of following a track, they'd trek through thick forests and snowstorms, over icy mountains and frozen rivers. They'd face below-zero temperatures, lonely tundra, and wild animals. These extreme conditions and some of the world's toughest terrain make for a race that even Olympians would be hard-pressed to survive. It's the "Last Great Race on Earth," better known as the Alaskan Iditarod.

Each year on the first Saturday in March, the world's greatest dog teams race from Anchorage in central Alaska to Nome on the coast of the Bering Sea. Today, the dogs' drivers, or mushers, can win thousands of dollars in cash and prizes. But back in 1925, when dogs and mushers first raced along the Iditarod trail, the stakes were much higher.

Only the Dogs Could Save Them

The trail started out as a mail and supply route from Seward, in southeastern Alaska, to Nome, but in January 1925, it took on a more important role. Nome, Alaska— then a town of about 1,500 people—faced a deadly epidemic. Six children had already died of diphtheria when Dr. Curtis Welch, director of the U.S. Public Health Service and the only physician in the area, announced that without antitoxin serum, hundreds more children and adults would die. Particularly at risk was Nome's Native American population, which had no natural immunity to diphtheria.

There were about 300,000 units of antitoxin in Anchorage, enough to halt the epidemic, but the state was in the grip of winter. Most of the days were dark, blizzards ravaged the landscape, and temperatures were well below zero. The open-cockpit airplanes of the day couldn't make the trip, and the nearest railroad was in Nenana, 674 miles from Nome. The antitoxin traveled by train to Nenana, but from there, the sick residents had only one hope: the Alaskan sled dog teams.

Doctors set up a relay of dog teams and mushers to carry the medicine along a portion of the Iditarod trail from Nenana to Nome. The name Iditarod, comes from the native Alaskan term *haiditarod*, or "distant place." Indeed, the trail ran through some of the state's most forbidding wilderness and was nearly impassable in winter. But the dogs would have to travel it in record time.

On Your Mark, Get Set . . . Go!

Glass vials of the diphtheria antitoxin serum were packed into a cylindrical container that was wrapped in quilting, canvas, and furs and then sent off from Anchorage by train. At 9 p.m. on January 27, the 20-pound package arrived in Nenana. Musher "Wild Bill" Shannon packed it on his sled and set off. The temperature was 40 below zero and dropping.

Shannon's team was led by Blackie, a sturdy black-and-white dog whose grandfather was a timberwolf. Blackie led eight other dogs (most of them inexperienced) across a frozen river, through snowdrifts, and into winds that blew them right off their feet. For some of the time, Shannon jogged alongside the sled to keep warm, but when he arrived in the town of Minto at 3 a.m., he was suffering from frostbite and hypothermia. Shannon and his team rested and warmed up and then took off again a few hours later. This time, Blackie led a team of only five dogs—the other three were left behind in Minto, too exhausted to go on.

For the rest of the story, turn to page 129.

Doggy Details

Get to know dogs by the numbers.

1

Ranking of the Labrador retriever on the list of most popular domestic dogs in the United States, Canada, and the United Kingdom.

2

Times per year that most female dogs go into heat. Each heat lasts about 20 days.

12 days

Age at which most puppies' eyes open fully. It takes about two more weeks for their vision to develop completely.

15 years

Average dog's life span.

24

Percentage of dogs who receive formal obedience training.

39

Percentage of American homes with dogs living in them. That's about 73 million dogs total.

45 miles per hour

Speed at which a greyhound, the world's fastest dog, can run. The average dog runs about 20 miles per hour.

60 days

The gestation period for dogs.

85 beats per minute

The average dog's heart rate, about the same as the average human's.

101.2°F

A dog's normal body temperature.

200

Average pounds of pressure per square inch that a dog's jaw exerts. Large dogs exert more than 450 pounds per square inch. (A human jaw exerts about 150 pounds of pressure per square inch.)

319

Bones in a dog's body. They also have 42 permanent teeth.

14,000

Approximate number of years ago that the first dogs were domesticated.

Good Dog

These heroic dogs saved the day!

Blue

What he did: One evening in 2001, Ruth Gay of Fort Myers, Florida, was out walking her dog Blue when she accidentally slipped on some wet grass and fell. The 84-year-old woman couldn't get up, and no one heard her cries for help—except a 12-foot alligator that crawled out of a nearby canal. Gay probably would have been gator food if Blue hadn't been there to protect her. The 35-pound dog fought with the gator, snarling and snapping until the reptile finally turned tail and left. Then Blue ran home barking, alerting Gay's family that she was in trouble. Gay was saved. And Blue? He was treated for 30 puncture wounds. "It's amazing what an animal will do in a time of need," said the vet. "He's a pretty brave dog."

Trixie

What she did: In 1991, 75-year-old Jack Fyfe of Sydney, Australia, was home alone when he suffered a paralyzing stroke. Unable to move, he lay helpless, waiting for someone to discover him as the temperature outside climbed to

90 degrees. Fyfe was crying for water—and that's just what Trixie brought him. She found a towel, soaked it in her water dish, and then laid it across Fyfe's face so he could suck out the moisture. She repeated this every day until her water dish ran dry, then she dipped the towel in the toilet. After nine days, Fyfe's daughter stopped by and found him alive . . . thanks to Trixie.

Sadie

What she did: Michael Miller was walking Sadie when he had a massive heart attack. He was unconscious, but his hand was still wrapped around Sadie's leash. Sadie tried to revive him by licking his face. When that failed, the 45-pound dog began pulling the 180-pound man toward their home, a third of a mile away. For an hour and a half, Sadie labored; when she finally reached the back door, she howled until Miller's wife came out. Because of the dog's heroism, Miller recovered.

Dorado

What he did: On September 11, 2001, Omar Eduardo Rivera was working on the 71st floor of the World Trade Center's north tower. Rivera, who was blind, was at his

desk with his guide dog, a Labrador named Dorado. When the hijacked planes hit the building and chaos ensued, Rivera let go of Dorado's leash in the hope that the dog would be able to run down the stairs alone and escape. But Dorado stayed at his master's side, so Rivera took hold of the leash and let Dorado lead him to the stairwell. The two took the stairs slowly despite the panicked people around them. At one point, they were separated, and Rivera thought Dorado had gotten lost in the crowd. But a moment later, the trusty Labrador nudged his master's leg, and the two traveled down the remaining stairs and out to safety on the street.

To read about some naughty dogs, turn to page 77.
For more good dogs, turn to page 217.

* * *

Food Fit for a King

Throughout history, the very wealthy fed their dogs food that was much better than what most humans ate.

- Nineteenth-century Chinese Empress Tzu Hsi fed her Pekingese shark fins, quail breasts, and antelope milk.
- During the 1700s and 1800s, European nobility fed their dogs roast duck, cakes, and candies.
- Some European royals even gave their canines highly prized liquors.

All in a Day's Search

Dogs can be trained to do many jobs, but few are more important than search-and-rescue. Here are eight things you may not know about search-and-rescue dogs.

1. Most search dogs are recruited from animal shelters. Their breed doesn't matter. German shepherds, Labs, golden retrievers, and bloodhounds are the best known animals used for search-and-rescue, but Border collies, bulldogs, and even mutts also do well.

2. Agility and persistence are two important personality traits in a search dog. These animals need to be . . . well . . . dogged. They're successful because they don't give up.

3. Search dogs were used to sniff out bombs and land mines as early as World War II. They were trained to locate metal.

4. Search dogs are not trained to attack, even when they're military dogs. They need to focus all their attention on tracking a scent, and must ignore any distractions, including possible attacks. It's their human handlers who are trained to watch out for danger so that the dogs can work.

5. Damp weather keeps a scent low to the ground and makes it easier for the dogs to track, so rain and fog are ideal conditions for a search.

6. Dogs are taught to specialize. Cadaver dogs look for remains but not live people. Rescue or "live find" dogs look for survivors. Other dogs zero in on particular smells. If something's got an odor, a dog can be trained to track it down.

7. A nasty rumor spread back in the 1970s that cadaver dogs would tear into their "finds" if not stopped. But that's untrue. Like any other type of search, once the dog finds something, he barks and waits to be rewarded.

8. Cadaver dogs are trained to sniff out human blood and skin, but no state allows people to buy body parts, making training these animals a challenge. Trainers resort to all sorts of tricks to teach their dogs to look for human remains—they'll even prick their own fingers to leave blood for the dogs to find.

Underdog Is Here

He's one of animation's most enduring characters and the first real hero to be tied to a product. Here's the skinny on the link between a kids' breakfast cereal and the popular crime-fighting canine Underdog.

Born in the Boardroom

The year was 1960, and General Mills—maker of Cheerios, Lucky Charms, and other popular children's cereals—was looking for a way to increase sales. The company's execs hired a New York ad agency called Dancer Fitzgerald Sample to figure out a way to do it. W. Watts Biggers, an account supervisor who'd started his career with the agency as an intern in the mail room, took the job.

Biggers teamed up with three others: writers Chester Stover and Treadwell Covington, and an artist named Joseph Harris. They asked themselves a couple of questions: Who's most likely to eat General Mills cereals? (Kids!) And what's the best way to communicate with those children? (Television!) So they decided to create a cartoon that would be sponsored by General Mills. Ads for GM cereals would run during commercial time, of course.

Doggone Brilliant

Biggers came up with a canine superhero, one who had powers like Superman but who also made mistakes and was silly, like kids. He named the hero "Underdog" and gave him a secret identity: Shoeshine Boy. Shoeshine didn't have any inborn superpowers; he was just a regular, lovable pooch. But when danger was on the horizon, he dashed to a phone booth, changed into his crime-fighting outfit (tights and a cape), took an Underdog Super Energy Vitamin Pill, and voilà! He turned into a superhero and uttered the phrase, "Never fear. Underdog is here!"

The vitamin pill was key to Underdog's powers. Without it, he was just a common hound. With it, though, he could move planets, defeat bad guys, and fly. So he always kept a spare in a ring on his finger . . . just in case.

Hitting the Airwaves

Biggers and his team finished the first cartoons in early 1964, and the first installment ran on NBC in October, with Wally Cox (of *Mr. Peepers* and *Beverly Hillbillies* fame) voicing the title character. *Underdog* was an instant hit. Kids loved the silly canine crime-fighter, and General Mills loved how many kids were being exposed to their cereal commercials.

With a successful cartoon under their belts, Biggers and his team left Dancer Fitzgerald Sample and formed their own company, Total TeleVision Productions. They took *Underdog* with them, and the show became one of the company's most successful ventures. Total TeleVision created and produced several children's cartoon series, including *Tennessee Tuxedo and His Tales* and *Tooter Turtle*, but when General Mills pulled its sponsorship in 1969, Total TeleVision folded.

The Dog with Nine Lives

Underdog, however, found a home in syndication. The show ran on NBC until 1973; it was revived in the 1980s and ran into the 1990s. The heroic canine also appeared in a 2007 live-action movie, and he's been a Macy's Thanksgiving Day Parade balloon since 1965.

Censored!

When *Underdog* ran in syndication during the 1980s and 1990s, scenes of him taking his Super Energy Vitamin Pill were removed. No official word was given, but angry fans cried censorship, saying the scenes were dropped in an attempt to make sure that NBC and the show couldn't be accused of promoting drug use.

To read about more animated TV canines, turn to page 192.

* * *

Since it was founded in 1995, the American Kennel Club's Canine Health Foundation has provided more than $15 million for canine health research.

Dog Food for Thought

*Take heed of these wise words from some
of the world's most famous dog lovers.*

"He that lieth down with dogs shall rise up with fleas."
—*Benjamin Franklin*

"If dogs could talk, it would take a lot of the fun out of owning one."

—*Andy Rooney*

"You may have a dog that won't sit up, roll over or even cook breakfast, not because she's too stupid to learn how but because she's too smart to bother."
—*Rick Horowitz, columnist*

"What counts is not necessarily the size of the dog in the fight; it's the size of the fight in the dog."
—*Dwight D. Eisenhower*

"Life is like a dogsled team: If you ain't the lead dog, the scenery never changes."

—*Lewis Grizzard, humorist*

"The more I see of men, the more I like dogs."

—*Madame de Stael,*
18th-century French activist

"I hope if dogs ever take over the world and they choose a king, they don't just go by size, because I bet there are some Chihuahuas with some good ideas."

—*Jack Handey, humorist*

"Yesterday I was a dog. Today I'm a dog. Tomorrow I'll probably still be a dog. Sigh! There's so little hope for advancement."

—*Snoopy*

"Don't accept your dog's admiration as conclusive evidence that you are wonderful."

—*Ann Landers*

"If you think dogs can't count, try putting three dog biscuits in your pocket and then giving Fido only two of them."

—*Phil Pastoret, author*

For more quotes, turn to page 177.

His Perfect Name

*A survey by Veterinary Pet Insurance listed these at the
30 most popular male dog names in the United States.*

1.	Max	16.	Shadow
2.	Buddy	17.	Rusty
3.	Jake	18.	Murphy
4.	Rocky	19.	Sammy
5.	Bailey	20.	Zeus
6.	Buster	21.	Riley
7.	Cody	22.	Oscar
8.	Charlie	23.	Winston
9.	Bear	24.	Casey
10.	Jack	25.	Tucker
11.	Toby	26.	Teddy
12.	Duke	27.	Gizmo
13.	Lucky	28.	Samson
14.	Sam	29.	Oliver
15.	Harley	30.	Bandit

Her Perfect Name

And now, the ladies. Find a name for your pet, or see where your dog's name ranks.

1.	Molly	16.	Abby
2.	Maggie	17.	Roxy
3.	Daisy	18.	Missy
4.	Lucy	19.	Brandy
5.	Sadie	20.	Coco
6.	Ginger	21.	Annie
7.	Chloe	22.	Katie
8.	Bailey	23.	Samantha
9.	Sophie	24.	Casey
10.	Zoe	25.	Gracie
11.	Princess	26.	Rosie
12.	Bella	27.	Misty
13.	Angel	28.	Emma
14.	Lady	29.	Sandy
15.	Sasha	30.	Heidi

A Serviceman's Best Friend

*Make no bones about it, this little guy was
one of America's greatest soldiers.*

Stubby Ships Out

A pit bull terrier appeared on the Yale Field in New
Haven, Connecticut, in the spring of 1917. Members of
the Connecticut National Guard, training on the field for
service in World War I, adopted him and named him
"Stubby" after his short stub of a tail. One soldier in particular—J. Robert Conroy—became very attached to Stubby,
and when the Guard headed overseas in July 1917, Conroy
refused to abandon his canine friend. He smuggled Stubby
aboard ship and brought him to Europe.

By February 5, 1918, Stubby was on the front lines. He
spent a year and a half there and saw action in 17 battles,
including the conflicts at Aisne-Marne, Champagne-
Marne, St. Mihiel, and Meuse Argonne in France. He
even learned to salute, putting his right paw on his right
eyebrow when the soldiers around him saluted.

Rear Guard

In every battle, Stubby proved invaluable to his soldier pals.

He carried messages through enemy lines, became expert at finding (and comforting) wounded men, and proved to be better than the men at predicting when enemy shells were headed their way. So the soldiers followed his lead when it came time to dive into the trenches. Once, Stubby even saved his regiment from a surprise mustard gas attack. In the middle of the night, at the first whiff of gas, he roused the sleeping soldiers, giving them time to don their gas masks, thus saving their lives.

But Stubby's most famous act of heroism involved his teeth. One night, while resting in a dugout with Stubby, Conroy awoke to hear the dog growl and saw him jump from the trench. Next, Conroy heard a human scream and sounds of a fight. The soldier grabbed his rifle and leaped out of the trench, where he found Stubby determinedly attached to the rear end of a German soldier who'd been spying in the Allied trenches. Stubby's heroic chomp on that rump made headlines in every major U.S. newspaper.

He Had the World by the Tail

Ultimately, "Sergeant Stubby" became one of the most honored and decorated soldiers of World War I. He was awarded a Purple Heart and several other medals, and his loyal, good nature earned him fans around the world. (After Stubby helped liberate Chateau Thierry from the Germans, a group of local French women made a blanket for him that incorporated the flags of all the Allied nations.)

When the war ended, Stubby visited with President

Woodrow Wilson and participated in a "welcome home" parade. In 1921, President Warren G. Harding invited Stubby to the White House, where General John Pershing awarded the dog with a gold victory medal.

The dog chocked up another honor when he was chosen to be a mascot at Georgetown University, where Conroy attended law school in 1922 and 1923. During halftime at Georgetown football games, Stubby pushed the ball around the field with his nose.

A Stout Legacy

Stubby died in 1926, but he left a permanent mark on history. His service helped the American military realize how useful dogs could be in war. During World War I, America's allies, as well as her enemies, had used thousands of dogs to carry messages and aid wounded soldiers. But the U.S. Army had no military training program for canines. Stubby's heroism inspired the military to start the American K-9 Corps that trained the dogs used in World War II, the Korean War, the Vietnam War, and the Middle Eastern conflicts. Many American soldiers have said that they owe their lives and safe return to brave dogs in the K-9 Corps. It's all just part of a day's work for heroes like Sergeant Stubby.

To read about more military dogs, turn to page 122.

Hollywood Hounds

Many movies have been made starring man's best friend, but a few pooches are silver-screen favorites. Can you identify them?

1. This clever terrier accompanied the martini-swilling Nick and Nora Charles on their screwball adventures in 1934's The Thin Man.

A. Asta

B. Shasta

C. Moe

2. This slobbering hound belonged to a cop (played by Tom Hanks) who acquired the dog after its previous owner was murdered.

A. Bob

B. Felix

C. Hooch

3. In his first movie, this golden retriever demonstrated an amazing ability to play basketball. In the film's sequels, the character learned to play football, baseball, volleyball, and soccer.

A. Sammy

B. Buster

C. Buddy

4. Named after a composer, this runaway puppy grows into a family's lovable Saint Bernard.

A. Mozart

B. Chopin

C. Beethoven

5. The first dog to play this canine character was named Pal; his owner bought him for $5 in 1941. Two years later, he starred his first movie and made $250 a week.

A. Lassie

B. Rin Tin Tin

C. Balto

6. This sandy-haired mutt starred in five films and four television projects during the 1970s and 1980s. In his first film, he becomes a hero who saved two children from a kidnapper.

A. Benji

B. Lassie

C. Rover

7. This dog first appeared in Willie Morris's memoir about growing up in Mississippi during the 1940s. In 2000, the book became a film and starred an English fox terrier named Enzo as the title character.

A. Old Yeller

B. Balto

C. Skip

For answers, turn to page 224.

Bark Like an Egyptian

Typically, cats are considered the most revered
pet in ancient Egypt, but the Egyptians loved
dogs, too. Take a look at the evidence.

The Proof's in the Paint

Paintings and carvings that decorate the Egyptian pharaohs'
tombs speak to the fact that the ancient Egyptians not only
owned dogs, they loved them. The earliest known Egyptian
carving of a dog is on a 6,000-year-old bowl; it shows a man
hunting with four leashed canines that look like greyhounds.
Later paintings and bas-reliefs depict a variety of dogs wearing collars, indicating that they're pets. Some have short legs
like dachshunds, others resemble mastiffs, but slender greyhounds are the most common. And many pieces of Egyptian
art show dogs hunting, shepherding flocks, or sitting at the
side of their masters. Even King Tutankhamen's famous tomb
held paintings and bas-reliefs showing him with his favorite
hunting dogs.

Pharaoh's Best Friend

Dogs have also been found entombed with their royal masters. One doggy grave at Giza (the site of the Pyramids)
even has an inscription naming the pet: Abuwitiyuw. The
pharaoh in the tomb remains unnamed, but the ruler
loved his dog Abuwitiyuw so much that he had the animal

buried in a royal coffin filled with luxuries: linen, incense, and perfumed ointment.

Of course, it wasn't just pharaohs who were buried with their pets. A museum at the University of Pennsylvania displays the mummy of a dog next to that of a commoner named Hapi-Men. The two mummies were found side-by-side in Hapi-Men's tomb.

Hey, Mummy!

The fact that the ancient Egyptians mummified dogs shows how important the animals were; in Egypt, being mummified was an honor. Archaeologists have found hundreds of dog mummies buried in many cemeteries from Abydos to Saqqara. They're a mix of breeds: large, small, greyhounds, mutts, even some jackals.

* * *

The Ancient Saluki

The dog most often linked to Egypt is the saluki, but the breed didn't originate there. Salukis are actually older than the Pyramids themselves, and images of them have been found in Sumerian carvings (in modern-day Iraq) that date to 6,000 B.C. Over the years, the breed's looks and skills haven't changed much. Sleek like a greyhound, the saluki can run up to 40 miles per hour. And its sharp eyes can spot animals moving a mile away. According to some experts, any dogs mentioned in the Old Testament were probably salukis.

Dog Park Etiquette 101

*Whether you're a new dog owner or an
old pro, take heed of the rules at the dog park.*

1. Always clean up after your dog, and never leave him unattended.

2. Toys start fights—don't bring them.

3. Make sure your dog is healthy before he hits the park. His shots should be up-to-date, and you never want to take a sick or flea-infested dog to the park.

4. Practice calling your dog to you during playtime so that he'll behave at the park.

5. Don't let your dog rush to the entrance every time a new dog arrives.

6. If your female dog is in heat, don't take her to the park.

7. Be prepared for messy dog play—bring towels for cleaning up.

8. Always have treats on hand . . . just in case.

Leading the Blind

*It may seem like a modern partnership, but dogs have been
helping the blind since the earliest days of canine domestication.
Here's a timeline of the history of guide dogs.*

A Long, Long Time Ago

Archaeologists in western Italy have found a first-century
mural in the buried ruins of the Roman city of Herculaneum
that shows a dog helping a blind man walk. And a wooden
plaque from the Middle Ages shows a dog on a leash leading
a blind man.

1780

Informal training for guide dogs began around 1780 at Les
Quinze-Vingts, a school for the blind in Paris. The school,
started by Valentin Haüy (known as "the Father and
Apostle of the Blind"), experimented with ways of teaching dogs and blind people to work together. But because
the school's focus was on education rather than mobility,
the guide dog training took a backseat.

1788

Josef Riesinger, a blind sieve maker from Vienna, trained his
spitz (a wolflike dog typically used for hunting, herding, and
pulling sleds) to help him walk and take part in other

daily activities. The dog was so well trained that people often doubted that Riesinger was blind.

1819

Johann Wilhelm Klein, the founder of Vienna's Institute for the Education of the Blind, wrote a book called the *Textbook for the Instruction of the Blind Ones*, which mentioned employing dogs to help blind people. There's no evidence, though, that Klein's techniques were ever used.

1847

Almost 30 years later, a Swiss man named Jakob Birrer wrote his own book: *Memories, Special Life Travels and Opinions of Jakob Birrer*. It told about his life experiences as a blind man, including what it was like to use a guide dog.

Early 1900s

Finally, when thousands of soldiers returned from World War I blinded by poison gas, the modern guide dog story began. German physi-

cian Gerhard Stalling got the idea to train dogs for the blind by chance. According to legend, he was called away while he and one of

his blind patients were taking a walk. Stalling left his dog with the patient, and when he returned, he saw that the dog appeared to be helping the patient move around. This led him to explore ways to train dogs as guides. In 1916, he opened the world's first guide dog school for the blind in Oldenburg, Germany. For the next 10 years, Stalling and his staff trained as many as 600 dogs a year.

By the mid-1920s, at least one other training facility had opened in Germany, and these schools inspired an American woman named Dorothy Harrison Eustis to write an article about the institutions for *The Saturday Evening Post*.

To read about Eustis and the school she created to teach dogs and blind students to work together, turn to page 119.

* * *

Runaway Dog

On her way home to California the day after winning an Award of Merit medallion at the 2006 Westminster Dog Show, a three-year-old whippet named Vivi escaped from her crate after check-in at JFK Airport. Wearing only a black doggy sweater, Vivi was last seen sprinting down a runway into the cold Queens night. She was never found, although sightings continue to this day.

Delta Airlines eventually ponied up its legal liability of $2,800 for the dog (considered to be worth $20,000), plus another $2,000 toward the cost of the search.

Dogs in Space

When people think of dogs and the Soviet space program, most only remember Laika, who died in orbit. But actually, many dogs were launched into space during the early years of the Soviet program, and most of them made it home safely.

Early Astronauts

In the early 1950s, the Soviet Union placed dogs aboard several suborbital rocket flights, something no other nation did for test flights. Soviet scientists chose dogs because they believed the animals were hardy, trainable, and likely to remain calm during the launch-and-return process. These early flights traveled just over 62 miles—to the internationally accepted boundary of space—and then fell back to Earth.

The first pups to make the trip were Dezik and Tsygan, a pair of mixed-breed strays. They flew in July 1951 aboard a Russian rocket called the R-1. The animals were safely recovered by parachute after they traveled 60 miles through the atmosphere.

In all, the Soviet Union used more than a dozen dogs for its suborbital test flights. Most of the animals flew on more than one mission. Otvazhnaya (Brave One), however, was a notable repeat astronaut who flew on five suborbital test flights and was later honored on a Romanian stamp.

Lost Laika

Laika, of course, was the first living being launched into orbit. Her real name was Kudryavka, which meant "Little Curly." She was a mixed breed with husky and Samoyed features. This type of dog, the mixed-breed hunter, is called *laika* in Russian, and Western media outlets picked up on that name. She was also nicknamed "Muttnik" by the American press.

Laika died while in orbit on *Sputnik 2* in 1957, but her groundbreaking role in space exploration led her to be honored in many ways. Her image appeared on Russian stamps. Her statue is included on the Monument to the Conquerors of Space in Moscow. And mission controllers of the Mars Exploration Rover *Opportunity* named a region on Mars after her.

Upward and Onward

After Laika's death, the Soviets made it a priority to test sending more living creatures into space and bringing them back again. Between 1957 and 1961, dogs led the way. Belka and Strelka (Squirrel and Little Arrow) both flew aboard *Sputnik* 5 and spent a day in space before returning home. This made them the first living creatures to make a round-trip voyage to space. Strelka eventually had six puppies, and Soviet Premier Nikita Khrushchev gave one of them, Pushinka, to President John F. Kennedy's daughter, Caroline. (Pushinka had puppies as well, and Kennedy called them "pupniks.")

Even after human beings were regularly flying into space, dogs went too. On the Soviet spacecraft *Cosmos 110*, Veterok (Little Wind) and Ugolyok (Little Lump of Coal) spent 22 days in orbit in 1966. (Humans didn't spend that much time in space until four years later.) Veterok and Ugolyok still hold the canine record for the longest time spent in space.

* * *

Calling All Coon Dogs

If you're ever near Tuscumbia, Alabama, you can check out the Coon Dog Cemetery. Back in 1937, a local named Key Underwood buried his coon dog Troop in the meadow where the cemetery now sits. He marked the grave with a rock and used a hammer and screwdriver to engrave Troop's name into the stone. That might have been the end of the story had Troop not been known as one of the most loyal and skilled hunting dogs around. Other hunters were touched by the gesture and started burying their coon dogs nearby.

Today, more than 150 coon dogs rest there, and the cemetery accepts this breed only: Underwood said in a 1985 interview that no hunter would want to "contaminate this burial place with poodles and lap dogs." The graves are marked with headstones—some made of sheet metal, some of wooden slabs, others of actual stone—and many include poignant epigraphs. Our favorite: "He was good as the best, and better than the rest." RIP.

The Westminster Dog Show By the Numbers

Every February, New York City goes to the dogs when 2,500 of the finest canines in the world strut their stuff in Madison Square Garden at the annual Westminster Kennel Club Dog Show.

2

Number of days the show lasts, always on the second Monday and Tuesday in February.

3

Number of times the first Best in Show winner, a smooth fox terrier named Warren Remedy, won the title (1907, 1908, and 1909). Six other dogs have won it twice, the most recent being an English springer spaniel named Chinoe's Adamant James in 1971 and 1972.

4 pounds

Weight of the smallest Best in Show winner, a Pomeranian named Great Elms Prince Charming II, who won in 1988. The largest was Seaward's Blackbeard, a 155-pound Newfoundland who took the title in 1984.

6

Number of "benched" dog shows in the United States. (Westminster is one.) A benched show is one in which the dog contestants must stay in their assigned bench area for the duration of the show unless they are in the ring, exercising, or being groomed. This makes them available to meet and greet the throngs of spectators who attend the show each year.

8

Maximum number of words a dog competing in the show can have in his or her name.

9 months

Age of the youngest dog to win Best in Show: a rough collie named Laund Loyalty took the title in 1929. The oldest dog (a papillon named Loteki Supernatural Being who won in 1999) was 8 years, 1 month, and 10 days old.

$40

General admission to the show; $125 will get you an assigned seat.

65

Percent of Best in Show winners who have have been males.

99

Best in Show titles awarded between 1907 (when the

award was introduced) and 2007. (There was no Best in Show winner in 1923 because the American Kennel Club was amending its rules). Forty-four of those titles have been taken by a terrier.

165

Number of American Kennel Club recognized breeds and varieties represented at the 2007 show. The winner from each breed goes on to compete for the best in its group: Sporting, Hound, Working, Terrier, Toy, Non-Sporting, and Herding. The seven group winners then compete for the Best in Show title.

1,201

Contestants who participated in the first Westminster Dog Show in 1877. That first show was held in the Hippodrome at Gilmore's Garden, an early incarnation of Madison Square Garden. The show was founded by a group of sport hunters who used to meet for drinks in Manhattan's Westminster Hotel and swap stories about the talents of their hunting dogs. The men decided to increase the competition and create a contest for bragging rights, so they formed a club—the Westminster Kennel Club—organized the first show, and offered prizes (like pearl-handled pistols) to the winners.

1888

Year that Anna Whitney, the first woman to serve as a

judge in an American dog show, participated at Westminster. In 1933, M. Hartley Dodge was the first woman to judge Best in Show.

2,632
Contestants in the 2007 show. There were 2,500 dogs entered in the breed competition and 132 in Junior Showmanship, where young dog handlers compete on their ability to show—or "handle"—their dogs.

$100,000
Estimated average cost to purchase, raise, and train a show-quality dog.

10 million
Average number of viewers who tune in to the USA Network each year to watch the crowning of the Westminster Best in Show.

* * *

Canine Celebrations
Another Westminster tradition takes place the day after the show. At the victory lunch at New York's Sardi's restaurant, where the Best in Show winner receives a celebratory meal: filet mignon served on a silver platter.

The Dog-Walk of Fame

*Since wolves first managed to sit and stay with humans
some 15,000 years ago, humans have prized canines for
their loyalties. Here are some four-legged friends who
deserve stars on the doggy Walk of Fame.*

Till Death Do Us Part

Greyfriars Bobby was the scrappy Skye terrier companion
of John Gray, a night watchman who lived in Edinburgh,
Scotland, in the mid-1800s. No matter the weather or the
time of year, Bobby faithfully accompanied his master on
his nightly rounds. When Gray died of tuberculosis in
1858 and was buried in Greyfriars Kirkyard, Bobby spent
much of time by his master's graveside. Bobby lived in the
cemetery for 14 years and left only to eat. Waiters at a
local restaurant, the Coffee House—a favorite haunt of
John Gray—fed him lunch each day.

The dog died in 1872, and a wealthy baroness, touched
by his story, paid for a statue to be erected in his honor in
Edinburgh. Bobby was buried inside the gate of Greyfriars
Kirkyard, but not in the cemetery itself—dogs weren't
allowed to be buried on sacred ground in those days. (John
Gray's grave is nearby.) Today, a monument marks Bobby's
grave; it reads, "Let his loyalty and devotion be a lesson to
us all."

Bobbie, Come Home!

Bobbie was a Scottish collie/English shepherd mix, owned by the Brazier family of Silverton, Oregon. In 1923, while in Indiana on vacation with the family, Bobbie was attacked by a pack of dogs and ran away. The Braziers searched for days for their beloved pet, but when all their efforts proved fruitless, the brokenhearted family drove back to Oregon without him. Six months later, Bobbie turned up in Silverton—2,800 miles from where he'd gotten lost. He was exhausted and scrawny, and his feet were badly worn. But he was alive and had somehow managed to find his way home.

Bobbie's story made him famous. He got a steak-and-cream dinner, a silver collar, a luxury doghouse, and keys to the city of Silverton. He became the subject of newspaper articles, books, and films; he even appeared in an article for *Ripley's Believe It or Not*. And when he died in 1927, Rin Tin Tin (who found fame in the movies) laid a wreath on his grave.

Man's Best Friend

In 1869, in Warrensburg, Missouri, a local sheep farmer named Samuel Ferguson shot and killed Old Drum, Charles

Burden's beloved hunting dog. Ferguson claimed Old Drum had trespassed on his landlord's property, but Burden disagreed and sued the landlord. During the trial, his lawyer, George Graham Vest, delivered an address in which he said, "The one absolutely unselfish friend that a man can have in this selfish world . . . is his dog."

According to reports of the time, the jury members had tears in their eyes when Vest finished his speech. They also decided in Burden's favor and awarded him damages of $500. Today, a statue of Old Drum stands outside the Warrensburg courthouse.

Faithful Dog Hachiko

Hachiko was the name of a male Akita puppy adopted in 1923 by Professor Eisaburo Ueno of Tokyo University. Every day, the professor took the train to work. When he returned each evening, Hachiko met him at the Shibuya Station, and they walked home together. One day, the professor suffered a stroke at work and died instantly.

Each day for the next 10 years, Hachiko waited for his master at the station. At first, he walked several miles daily from the farm of relatives who adopted the dog after the professor died. But eventually, Ueno's gardener, who lived close to the station, took Hachiko in. Over the years, Hachiko's story was published in newspapers all over Japan, and the dog became a symbol of family loyalty and devotion.

Hachiko died in 1935. Today, a bronze statue of Ueno's loyal friend stands in Shibuya Station, and each April, local residents still hold a special ceremony to honor the faithful Akita.

Juneau's Official Greeter

Patsy Ann was an English bull terrier who lived in Juneau, Alaska, in the 1930s and 1940s. She was born deaf, but was somehow able to sense when a ship was pulling into port. Sometimes, she knew it before anyone on land could actually see the vessel. And for each ship, Patsy Ann would trot over to the dock, sniff the portholes (the sailors usually offered her treats), and greet the people arriving in Juneau.

She became a town celebrity and was featured on postcards and souvenirs. She put her paw prints in the cement of South Seward Street, and she earned her keep by making daily visits to local shops, restaurants, and hotels for snacks and treats. (Tourists loved to feed her too.) For 13 years, Patsy Ann was a fixture in Juneau, and when she died in 1942, a crowd of mourners gathered while locals lowered her small coffin into the sea. Patsy Ann may be gone, but a statue of her stands at the harbor and greets visitors as she once did.

* * *

Hardy Har-Har

Q: Why can dogs scratch whenever they want to?
A: They live in a flea country.

Chow Down

Ever wonder what your pooch would have eaten 200 years ago?
Here's the history of the multi-billion-dollar dog food industry.

Kibble: The Early Years

For centuries, dog owners have been offered advice on feeding their pets. More than 2,000 years ago, Roman poet and philosopher Marcus Terentius Varro wrote the first farming manual. In it, he advised farmers to give their dogs barley bread soaked in milk and bones from dead sheep. During the Middle Ages, European royals hired kennel cooks to make huge stews for their hounds. The stews were made mostly from grains and vegetables with some meat or meat by-products—the hearts, livers, and lungs of various livestock.

Dogs in common households, though, had meager diets. They were fed only what their owners could spare. A typical diet consisted of crusts of bread, bare bones, potatoes, cabbage, or whatever they could scrounge on their own.

Things started to change in the mid-1800s, when the Industrial Revolution created a middle class that had more money and more leisure time than their ancestors. Pets began to be regarded as luxury items by everyday folk, and as a result, pet food was closely scrutinized. Many people argued that dogs needed to be "civilized." Since wild dogs ate raw meat, domesticated dogs shouldn't. (That advice influenced the pet food industry for decades after.)

Dog Cakes

In the late 1850s, James Spratt—a young electrician from Cincinnati, Ohio—got an idea when he sailed to London to sell lightning rods. When his ship arrived, crewmen threw the leftover "ship's biscuits" (or hardtack) onto the dock, where they were devoured by hordes of waiting dogs. Ship's biscuits were made with flour, water, and salt that was mixed into a stiff dough, baked, and left to harden and dry. The biscuits were easily stored and had a long shelf life, which was important in the days before refrigeration. They also looked a lot like today's dog biscuits.

Spratt had the idea that he could make cheap, easy-to-serve biscuits and sell them to the growing number of urban dog owners. His recipe: a baked mixture of wheat, beetroot, and vegetables bound together with beef blood. When Spratt's Patent Meal Fibrine Dog Cakes came on the market in England in 1860, they were a success. Ten years later, he took the business to New York, and the American pet food industry was born.

A Growing Trend

Others followed in Spratt's footsteps:

- The F. H. Bennett Company opened in 1908, making biscuits shaped like bones. Bennett also made the first puppy food and was the first to package different-sized kibble for different breeds.
- In 1931, Nabisco bought Bennett's company and renamed the biscuits Milk-Bones. Then the company hired 3,000 salesmen to get Milk-Bones into food stores.
- In 1922, Chappel Brothers of Rockford, Illinois, introduced Ken-L Ration, the first canned dog food in the United States. In 1930, they started sponsoring a popular radio show, *The Adventures of Rin Tin Tin*.

Aw, Dry Up

By 1941, 90 percent of dog food in the United States was canned. But then the United States entered World War II, and the government started rationing tin and meat. Shortly thereafter, dry dog food became popular again.

In 1950, the Ralston Purina Company started using a new machine to make its Chex cereal. Here's how it worked: ingredients were pushed through a tube, cooked under high pressure, and puffed up with air. This allowed Chex to stay crisp when milk was added. At about the same time, manufacturers were getting complaints about the appearance, texture, and digestibility of dry dog food. Purina's pet food division borrowed one of the machines from the cereal division and experimented with it in secret for three years. The result: Purina Dog Chow. Dogs loved it, it digested well, and it quickly became (and remains) the number-one dog food in the nation.

No People Food for You

In 1964, the Pet Food Institute—a lobbying group for the now-gigantic pet food industry—began a campaign to get people to stop feeding their dogs anything but packaged dog food. They funded reports that appeared in magazines and detailed the benefits of processed dog food. The institute even produced a radio spot about "the dangers of table scraps." Soon, the dog food industry was spending an incredible $50 million a year on advertising. Commercials centered around the "beef wars," with competing companies all claiming to have the most pure beef. (*Bonanza* star Lorne Greene even did a TV commercial for Alpo . . . holding a sirloin steak.) As a result, processed dog food replaced table scraps as the most popular way to feed America's canine population.

In the 1960s and 1970s, increasing numbers of dog breeds and rising crime rates made dog ownership skyrocket. By 1975, there were more than 1,500 dog foods on the market. Today, more than 1,600 square miles of soybeans, 2,100 square miles of corn, and 1.7 million tons of meat and poultry products are made into pet food every year. There are more than 70 million dogs in the United States, and pet food is an $11 billion industry . . . and it's still growing.

To read about the evolution of dog treats, turn to page 126.

The AKC's Good Citizens

Dogs in the American Kennel Club can earn Canine Good Citizen Certificates, which recognize pooches who pass a 10-step basic training test. The steps are as follows:

1. Accepting a friendly stranger
2. Sitting politely for petting
3. Appearance and grooming
4. Out for a walk (walk on a loose leash)
5. Walking through a crowd
6. Sitting and down on command/staying in place
7. Coming when called
8. Reaction to another dog
9. Reactions to distractions
10. Supervised separation

Pet Me

Quick bits of canine trivia for the dog lover in everyone.

- If your dog seems wary of the rain, it's not only because he doesn't want to get wet. Rain amplifies sound, and it hurts dogs' ears.

- Small dogs usually live longer than larger breeds: on average, about seven years longer. Tibetan terriers can live to be 20 years old.

- In ancient Rome, it wasn't officially dark until you could no longer tell the difference between a wolf and a dog in the distance.

- Average dog's annual vet bill: $300 to $500.

- In Japan, you can rent a dog as a companion for $20 an hour.

- Comedian John Candy once paid $19,000 for a German shepherd. (Apparently, he didn't know that the average price for a German shepherd was about $1,500.)

- Most popular dog names in Russia: Ugoljok (Blackie) and Veterok (Breezy).

- Elvis Presley owned seven dogs during his lifetime: Baba (collie), Getlo (chow), Muffin (Great Pyrenees), Sherlock (basset hound), Snoopy (Great Dane), Stuff (poodle), and Teddy Bear of Zixi Pom-Pom (poodle).

* * *

Guides to the Afterlife

Among many Native American tribes, dogs guide the spirits of the newly deceased on their way to the "Land of the Grandparents." In Native American culture, dogs are also linked with the powers of the sun and the moon. The association with the moon may have stemmed from dog's habit of howling at the moon, and the solar connection may come from dog's habit of walking around in circles before he lies down. To the Native Americans, this circling was equivalent to creating a symbol of the sun.

(Super)Man's Best Friend

What's a superhero without his superdog?

Rex the Wonder Dog

DC Comics' first heroic dog was never a superhero's companion. Rex the Wonder Dog debuted in a comic of the same name in January 1952; it ran twice a month for eight years. Rex was a German shepherd and a former member of the U.S. Army's K-9 Corps. He developed abilities beyond those of a normal dog when he was injected with an experimental super-soldier serum. In the comics, Rex could ride horses, swing on ropes, drive a stagecoach, and defeat foes from lions, wolves, and octopuses to a Tyrannosaurus rex. To top it off, Rex was also immortal because during one adventure, he sniffed out the Fountain of Youth.

The Dog of Steel

Superman may have been the last son of Krypton, but Krypto was the last dog. Originally, Krypto had the same powers as Superman—speed, strength, invulnerability, X-ray vision, super-hearing and smell, and the ability to fly. He first appeared in comic form in March 1955. According to the comic, Superman's father didn't just put his son in an untested rocket and send him to Earth. First, he tested the rocket on the family dog—Krypto. Krypto's rocket was knocked off course, though, and arrived on Earth when Clark Kent was a teenager. Krypto showed up in the Superman comics for years, moonlighting as the Kents' dog Skip. To preserve his secret identity, Krypto (who was born with white fur) dyed a patch of his fur brown when he was posing as Skip and used his X-ray vision to remove the spot when duty called. When he wasn't assisting Superman, Krypto zipped around the galaxy and visited distant planets. He communicated with Superman through "barking code," similar to Morse code.

When DC reworked all of its comics in the 1970s, Krypto mostly disappeared from Superman's story. The dog showed up occasionally, sometimes as an ordinary dog, sometimes as a super dog with limited powers. The TV show *Smallville*, about the teenaged Clark Kent, included an episode about Krypto in which he was a normal dog who was the victim of nefarious kryptonite experiments. In 2005, Krypto briefly stepped into the limelight with his own show, *Krypto the Superdog*, which aired on the Cartoon Network. But even though his name was in the title, the canine seemed fated to always play second fiddle to his human master; the show was canceled after just a year and a half.

The Bat-Hound

Batman got his own canine companion in June 1955. Ace, the Bat-Hound, was an ordinary German shepherd who sniffed out criminals, tracked down kidnappers, and otherwise accompanied Batman on his world-saving adventures. To prevent villains from identifying him as the pet of Bruce Wayne, Ace always wore a mask like his master's while on duty. And his dog collar bore the bat emblem.

Ace didn't last very long in the comics—he disappeared in 1964 (along with other extraneous characters, including the impish Bat-Mite). Since then, other dogs have appeared in the Batman comics, most notably Robin's telepathic dog Nighthound. The *Batman Beyond* animated TV series included a Great Dane named Ace who accompanied an older Bruce Wayne, but that Ace never wore a hood. Ace also showed up on *Krypto the Superdog* during its short run on the Cartoon Network; in that show, he wore a cape and used various gadgets just like Batman.

Other Crime-Fighting Fidos

- The original Manhunter, a cop trying to clear his brother's name, had a pet dog named Thor. Later on, it was revealed that Thor was actually a robotic sentry.
- The Phantom—sometimes called "the ghost who walks"—had a wolf companion named Devil.

- The Hanna-Barbera cartoon show *Super Friends*, which ran from 1973 to 1986, told the stories of the Justice League of America. In addition to Superman, Batman, Wonder Woman, and other comic heavy hitters, the Justice League had two teen sidekicks, Wendy and Marvin, and their pet, Wonderdog. After the first season, though, these three were replaced by the Wonder Twins, a brother and sister who could morph into any type of water or animal, respectively.

* * *

Oh, Blessed Pooch

Each October on the feast day of St. Francis of Assisi (patron saint of animals), Catholic churches around the world celebrate all creatures great and small. In the Philippines, for example, dogs (as well as an iguanas, pythons, and turtles) have been welcomed into a Manila church by Reverend Michael Martin for the annual blessing.

Episcopalians also have their dog days. At the St. Francis Episcopal Church in Stamford, Connecticut, Reverend Richard Mayberry's "flock" includes dogs (and some cats) who accompany their owners to church once a month to attend a special pet-friendly service. At these Sunday services, the readings and prayers honor the blessings that animals bring to humans.

Now That's Ugly!

Pride in one's dog takes many forms. How about the world's ugliest?

Westminster it's not, but at the Sonoma-Marin County Fair in Petaluma, California, the World's Ugliest Dog contest has been entertaining visitors for two decades. It started as a local summer attraction in 1988 but has garnered so much media attention over the years that now news cameras outnumber entrants, Internet voting climbs to the tens of thousands, and ugly aspirants travel from as far away as Florida to compete. (Winners get trophies, prize money, and the title, of course.) In 2006, suspense was especially high because Sam, the champion for three years running, had died at the age of 14, and the field was wide open for the 18 (really bad-looking) contenders. Here's a look at some of the ugliest winners ever to grace a dog show stage.

Sam
Awards: World's Ugliest Dog (2003, 2004, 2005)
Probably the most famous ugly dog, Sam was a 13-pound Chinese crested who was so ugly that his owner, Susie Lockheed, was scared of him when she first brought him home. (He was also so ugly that Japanese TV reporters

compared him to Godzilla.) Sam was acne-riddled, blind, warty, and hairless (unless you count the straggly wisps sticking out of his head). He had crooked teeth, a fatty tumor on his chest, and a line of moles down his nose. But Lockheed loved him. Sam came to her as a rescue dog; his original owner lost her pet-friendly apartment and could no longer keep him. Early in their relationship, Lockheed was diagnosed with cancer. Sam slept with her, comforted her, and saw her through chemotherapy, proving that judging an old dog on bad looks is never fair.

Cuddly side aside, he was plenty cranky, and had a fascination with his back leg. To Lockheed, it seemed that Sam believed there was an imaginary foe attached to his back leg. He'd snarl at it and bite, and whenever she gave him a treat, Sam would keep a close eye on that back leg to make sure it didn't steal the snack away.

TatorTot
Award: Ugliest Mutt (2005)
Sam may have gained worldwide fame for his hideousness, but his girlfriend—who is part Chihuahua, part Chinese crested—is pretty ill-favored, too. TatorTot, another dog belonging to Susie Lockheed, never did win the World's Ugliest title at the fair, but she did take Ugliest Mutt honors in 2005. TatorTot has her looks and personality working against her, it seems. She's only mostly hairless, not nearly as snarly as Sam, and has a tuft of white hair atop

her head. Apparently, says Lockheed, TatorTot is just too cute to take home the top prize.

Archie
Award: World's Ugliest Dog (2006)
In 2006, Archie (yet another Chinese crested) earned the title of World's Ugliest Dog. His owner, Heather Peoples, traveled all the way from Arizona to show off Archie's attributes at the fair. Unlike his predecessor, Archie does have hair—it sticks up erratically all over his head. His tongue hangs out of one side of his mouth because he has no teeth to hold it in place. His naked, liver-colored belly resembles a sausage. And he's so ugly that the animal shelter where he was living (and where Peoples worked) gave Peoples $10 to take him away. It was supposed to be just a temporary thing, but Peoples says her husband fell in love with the beauty-impaired beast: "Now when we go out, my husband carries Archie in his arms like a baby."

Archie was the winner in a year fraught with scandal. The ugliest dog is crowned after an Internet voting campaign that lasts several weeks, but during the 2006 process, computer hackers infiltrated the contest's Web site and erased votes from some of the top dogs. Fortunately, contest organizers discovered the crime and remedied the situation: they started the voting over from scratch. In the end, Archie pulled past favorites Munchkin, Rascal, and Pee Wee Martini to take the crown.

Elwood
Award: World's Ugliest Dog (2007)

This Chihuahua and Chinese crested mix took the top title after coming in second in 2006. He traveled all the way to California from New Jersey with his owner, Karen Quigley, who—despite the dog's new title—thinks Elwood is "the cutest thing that ever lived." Elwood's Internet voters, obviously, disagreed. With his dark, almost hairless body (Elwood does have a tuft of white fur atop his misshapen head) and a tongue that always droops from his mouth, Elwood is sometimes called "Yoda" or "ET"—affectionate nicknames, for sure. Besides winning the title and taking home $1,000, Elwood is somewhat of a local celebrity back home in New Jersey, where he's a Good Will Ambassador for the SPCA. He and Quigley try to educate people about special-needs pets (from sick animals to ugly ones) and encourage residents to adopt homeless dogs and cats.

* * *

Give Me Your (South)Paw

Ever notice that dogs prefer to "shake" with the same paw each time? According to tests made at the Institute for the Study of Animal Problems in Washington, dogs, like people, are either right- or left-handed—they favor either their right or left paws.

Your Royal Dogness

*When it comes to living a dog's life, it all depends
on the company you keep. Check out these treasured
royal breeds from around the world.*

China

More than 2,500 years ago, the dogs we call Pekingese
guarded the emperors of China. In the first century AD,
Emperor Ming Ti, a Buddhist, named them *Fu Lin*, or
"lion dogs." The lion represented strength to Buddhists—
but China had no lions, so Ming Ti wasn't sure what those
animals looked like. He decided that his ferocious little
guard dogs matched the descriptions of lions. The dogs
could be owned only by aristocrats living in the Forbidden
City, the royal court in Beijing. In the early days,
Westerners called Beijing "Peking," so today we call the
dogs Pekingese.

The Pekingese became the beloved companions of
China's royal court. Ladies carried them around, hidden in
their voluminous sleeves. The dogs also wore silk robes
and had their own staffs to groom and care for them.

Tibet

Lhasa Apsos were originally bred as guard dogs in Lhasa,
Tibet, more than 2,000 years ago. The little dogs have

exceptional hearing, are very smart, and have good people skills (they can often tell friend from foe instinctively). This made them a coveted breed among Tibetan monks. During the 1600s, assassins broke into the palace of Tibet's fifth Dalai Lama, killed his guards, and almost reached his bedchamber. Before they could attack him, the Dalai Lama's Lhasa Apsos began barking ferociously, which alerted more palace guards and saved their master's life. After that, the breed earned the nickname *Abso Seng Kye*, Tibetan for "barking lion sentinel dog." They were never sold, only given as presents. The first Lhasa apsos in the United States were gifts from the 13th Dalai Lama to C. Suydam Cutting, a naturalist from New Jersey who visited Tibet in the 1930s.

Tibet is also the birthplace of the Tibetan mastiff, a big dog that came to Europe during the Renaissance. The Tibetan mastiff became such a favorite of kings and queens that only they and nobles could own them.

Europe

Several breeds gained royal favor in Europe: After a pug saved the life of William of Orange, the breed became the official dog of his family, who ruled the Netherlands. Henry III of England and Francis I of France owned bichon frises and decked them out with ribbons and perfume. Great Pyrenees bore the royal arms of France in inscriptions 800 years old, and Russian czars favored Russian wolfhounds as early as the 13th century.

Greyhounds, though, had a special place in the hearts of Europeans. A law in England from around the 11th century states that "No meane person may keepe any greihounds."

Italian greyhounds—the breed's miniature version—came to Europe from Egypt 2,000 years ago, carried to Italy by Roman soldiers returning from military campaigns. Monarchs from England's Queen Victoria to Russia's Catherine the Great adored and kept them, but no one loved the little dogs more than Frederick the Great of Prussia. Frederick owned dozens of Italian greyhounds (all female), and slept with one or two favorites each night. They even went into battle with him. His favorite, Biche, was captured by the enemy at the Battle of the Sohr. Frederick sent one of his top generals to negotiate a prisoner exchange to get the dog back—a difficult task, since an enemy officer's wife had fallen in love with Biche and didn't want to return her. In the end, though, Biche came home to Frederick, who shed tears of joy when he saw her.

Honorable Mention: Japan

Akitas were first bred as hunting dogs back in the 17th century, when they were used to hold large game (boars, deer, and even bears) at bay until a hunter could arrive and make the kill. The animals are strong and hardy and have a thick coat to ward off the cold in the snowy mountains of Japan's Akita province, their homeland.

Akitas were once believed to have been so prized that

only Japan's royal family could own them. Dog fanciers claimed that elaborate rituals, costumes, and even a specialized language surrounded the Akita in Japanese history. The American Kennel Club bought into the story and printed it in guidebooks for many years, but today, most people are skeptical of the royalty claim because there's no recorded evidence to back it up.

Akitas came to the United States in 1937, when Helen Keller visited Japan and received one as a gift. The dogs weren't bred in America until after World War II, though, when U.S. soldiers—impressed with the animals' courage, intelligence, and loyalty—brought them home after tours of duty in Japan.

* * *

Why It's Great to Be a Dog

1. No one cares if you spend hours a day just smelling things.
2. Every garbage can looks like a buffet.
3. People consider your wet nose to be a sign of good health.
4. You don't have to take a bath every day, and no one expects you to brush your own hair.
5. You never have to pay for dinner.
6. If you gain weight or have rotten table manners, it's someone else's fault.
7. No one is offended if you scratch in public.

Proverbial Pooches

Dog proverbs show up in every culture on earth.
Here are some of our favorite sayings.

"If you are a host to your guest, be a host to his dog also."
—*Russia*

"To live long, eat like a cat, drink like a dog."
—*Germany*

"A house without either a cat or a dog is the house of a scoundrel."
—*Portugal*

"Children aren't dogs. Adults aren't gods."
—*Haiti*

"If you stop every time a dog barks, your road will never end."
—*Saudi Arabia*

"Only mad dogs and Englishmen go out in the noonday sun."
—*India*

"Every dog is allowed one bite."

—*United States*

"Three things it is best to avoid: a strange dog, a flood, and a man who thinks he's wise."

—*Wales*

"The dog's kennel is not the place to keep a sausage."

—*Denmark*

"The greater love is a mother's; then comes a dog's; then a sweetheart's."

—*Poland*

Famous for 15 Minutes

When Andy Warhol said, "In the future, everyone will be famous for 15 minutes," he probably didn't have dogs in mind. Yet even they haven't been able to escape the relentless publicity machine that keeps cranking out instant celebrities.

Dog Makes List of Notable Americans

The Star: Otis P. Albee, family dog of the Albees, in South Burlington, Vermont (breed unknown)

What Happened: In the 1980s, George Albee, a professor at the University of Vermont, was invited to submit biographical information for a book called *Community Leaders and Noteworthy Americans*. Instead, he filled out the forms for his dog—"a retired explorer, hunter and sportsman with a Ph.D. in animal husbandry."

Aftermath: Otis made it into the book. When this was reported nationwide, Albee announced that Otis had no comment. Apparently, neither did the book's publishers.

Nuts to Him! California Dog Wins Nutty Contest

The Star: Rocky, a 100-pound male Rottweiler

What Happened: In 1996, a Fresno radio station ran a contest offering free Neuticles to the dog who submitted the best ghostwritten essay on why he wanted them.

(Neuticles are artificial plastic testicles, implanted after a dog is neutered, that supposedly make the dog feel better about himself.) The appropriately named Rocky won.

Aftermath: The contest made national news. *Parade* magazine called it the "Best Canine Self-Improvement Story" of 1996.

A Dog Is Man's . . . Best Man?

The Star: Samson, a six-year-old Samoyed mix

What Happened: In 1955, Dan Anderson proposed to Lori Chapasko at the Wisconsin animal shelter where they both volunteered. She said yes . . . and approved when Dan chose their dog Samson to be "best man" at the wedding. "He epitomizes everything a best man should be," Anderson explained to reporters.

Aftermath: The dog's role was news, but apparently the wedding wasn't. Reporters seem to have ignored it.

* * *

A Dog Eat Emperor World

When Napoléon Bonaparte married Josephine de Beauharnais in 1796, he had to fight for his place in her heart. His rival? A possessive pug named Fortuné. The dog won several early battles by biting Napoléon on the leg, but Josephine adored the little animal, who even traveled in his own private carriage.

A Dog's Work

Plenty of dogs do traditional jobs: finding lost hikers or escaped criminals, searching through collapsed buildings or mudslides for survivors. But what does today's job market offer for dogs who crave the unusual? Here are four options for those career-minded canines.

Dogs can be taught to smell anything, even things like plastic or money, which seem to humans to have no odor at all. To make the grade, search dogs have to work with their trainers every day, learning to identify new smells and getting treats when they pick the right ones. It usually takes 10 to 14 months and several thousand dollars to train a good sniffer.

Heed Hollywood's Call

The Motion Picture Association of America hires dogs to sniff out undeclared (and possibly pirated) DVDs in airport luggage. (Actually, the dogs are trained to sniff out the polycarbonate plastic that DVDs are made of.) This job often involves travel to far-flung locations: DVD-sniffing Labs have been put to work at London's Heathrow Airport, shopping centers in the Philippines, warehouses in Malaysia, and border crossings in Asia. So far, all of the DVD-sniffing canines are from Ireland, where bomb-sniffing dogs are trained to find plastic explosives.

Go Buggy

From California to New York, fancy hotels hire dogs to sniff out bedbugs in their rooms. It takes a dog only minutes to locate the nasty insects that humans might never find until it's too late and the bugs have set up shop in somebody's luggage. (The hotels have gone to great pains to keep their names secret.) Once trained, a bug-sniffing dog can earn $200 per hour and can work for about six hours a day. Now that will pay for a lot of treats!

Play Matchmaker

Montana ranchers have started hiring dogs to sniff out which cows are in heat. Turns out that some canines are better at this than bulls. This career path is iffy, though. Veterinarians and ranchers still debate whether it makes economic sense to pay dogs to zero in on the cows' scent. After all, left to their own devices, the bulls usually catch on . . . eventually.

Fuzzy Mold Detectors

Dogs are three times better at detecting toxic mold in homes and buildings than any man-made instrument, so contractors have started hiring canines to sniff out the filthy fuzz. These dogs are specially trained to detect the 18 different varieties of toxic mold. Their owners earn anywhere from a few hundred to several thousand dollars per job, depending on the size of the building they inspect and the extent of the problems.

Designer Dogs

Twenty years ago, if a Labrador had mated with a poodle, the resulting offspring would be called a "mutt" or "mongrel." Today, such crossbreeds are incredibly popular and can cost thousands of dollars.

To Mix or Not to Mix?

To dog purists, mixing breeds contradicts the fundamental rationale for having purebreds: you know what to expect in regard to size, temperament, and instincts when the dogs grow up. Mixing two breeds creates offspring that are much less predictable. Also, the hybrid breeds are expensive. Puggles (a cross between a pug and a beagle) usually start at about $900, and Labradoodles can cost $2,000 to $3,000 each.

On the other side of the argument are people who say that purebred dogs are prone to genetic disorders like breathing issues (pugs), eye problems (cocker spaniels), and hip dysplasia (Saint Bernards and other large breeds). They argue that expanding the gene pool is a great idea because it breeds out these health problems and makes the animals physically stronger.

Call It What?

By far, the most common breed that people like to mix with others is the poodle. With their no-shed, no-dander, low-maintenance coat and high intelligence, poodles have become incredibly popular. But many breeds show up in the mix as well: Labradors, golden retrievers, Pekingese, basset hounds, and many others form the bases of new breeds. Here are some of the most popular (and most oddly named) mixes:

> **Labradoodle:** Labrador retriever and poodle
> **Cockapoo:** Cocker spaniel and poodle
> **Schnoodle:** Schnauzer and poodle
> **Goldendoodle:** Golden retriever and poodle
> **Yorkipoo:** Yorkshire terrier and poodle
> **Weimardoodle:** Weimaraner and poodle
> **Pekepoo:** Pekingese and poodle
> **Peagle:** Pekingese and beagle
> **Bagle:** Basset hound and beagle
> **Saint Berdoodle:** Saint Bernard and poodle
> **Sharp Asset:** Shar-Pei and bassett hound

Decoding Dogs

Body language is just as important a communication tool for dogs as it is for humans, and we wondered what dogs were trying to say when they exhibited certain behaviors. So we asked around, and here's what the experts told us.

Eyes and Eyebrows

- Dogs have a ridge above their eyes where their brows would be, and raising that ridge—like a human raising an eyebrow—means their interest is piqued. A furrowed brow suggests confusion or frustration.
- Half-moon eyes (when the whites of the eyes are showing in the shape of half-moons) warn that a dog prefers to not be bothered.
- Wide-open eyes indicate fear.
- A quick eye shift might be a signal of submission to another dog or human.
- Dogs who perceive a threat stare direct and hard at the offender. The offender just needs to look away for the tense encounter to end.

Mouth

- A dog who yawns or licks his lips when there's no food in sight is anxious.

- A pulled-back mouth (when it accompanies a relaxed face and energetic tail) means your dog is happy and excited.

Paws and Feet
- A dog who is lying down with one paw tucked beneath him is content.
- If he stands up and raises one paw, though, he wants to be left alone.
- Foot stamping from one paw to the other means your dog is excited and probably wants something. (This is most common before mealtime.)

Tails
- The higher the tail, the more confident the hound. A dominant dog will hold his tail straight up or just slightly curved over his back.
- Slow, small tail wags mean your dog is curious about his surroundings.
- A tail between the legs is a sign of anxiety.
- A fast-wagging tail means a dog is excited, but it doesn't necessarily mean he's friendly. If you come upon a dog with a fast-wagging tail who's staring you

down, back off. But if the dog's tail wags in big sweeps, his mouth and ears are relaxed, and his tongue is hanging out of his mouth, he probably just wants to play.

Full Body Communication

- When a dog crouches down with his rear in the air, he wants to play.
- If your dog flattens his ears, lowers his head and neck, and shifts his weight backward, it means he's ready to attack.
- When your dog arches his back downward and lowers his rear and head, he's showing a lack of confidence.
- A dog who rolls onto his back and exposes his stomach is taking on a submissive pose. It means he trusts you and accepts you as the dominant "dog."

* * *

Say Sorry, Charlie

In June 2007, a black Lab named Charlie took his owner for a spin. The dog jumped into Mark Ewing's Chevy Impala, knocked it into gear, and sent the car barreling down the driveway. Charlie jumped out pretty quickly, but the car plunged into a river down the hill. Ewing got a second dose of "this can't be happening to me!" when the local tow truck showed up. The tow truck operator had to dive into the river to hook up the car, but before he did, he asked Ewing to hold onto his dentures for safekeeping.

Scooby-Doo, Where Are You?

This bumbling canine may be the most popular TV cartoon dog ever.

House of Mystery

In 1969, Fred Silverman, the daytime programming director at CBS, asked TV's most prolific animators, Bill Hanna and Joe Barbera, to develop an animated series called *House of Mystery*. It was supposed to be a supernatural whodunit series based loosely on a combination of the 1940s radio show *I Love a Mystery* (considered by some critics to be the best radio serial ever) and the 1959–63 sitcom *Dobie Gillis*, which centered around a group of teenagers.

Hanna and Barbera quickly created some characters, but couldn't settle on a name for the show. They started with *Mysteries Five*, but then renamed it *Who's S-s-s-s-cared?* The plot revolved around four mystery-solving teenagers and their dog (who at that time had only a small part). Silverman took the idea to New York and presented it to the top CBS execs. To his surprise, they rejected it. The reason: it was too frightening for little children. That created a big problem for Silverman because he'd already reserved his best Saturday morning slot for the show. He was determined to change their minds.

The Chairman Comes Through

Silverman spent most of his flight back to Los Angeles trying to figure out how to sell the show. Finally, to relax, he put on his headphones. The first thing he heard was Frank Sinatra singing "Strangers in the Night," which ends with the nonsense lyrics "Scooby-Dooby-Doo."

Silverman suddenly had an inspiration—*that* could be the dog's name. And if he made the dog the star of the show, with the other characters supporting him, it would be funny rather than scary. The CBS executives bought it, and *Scooby Doo* was born.

Who's Who?

The final cast of characters included five principal players:

- Scooby-Doo, a Great Dane. Don Messick, who voiced everyone from Bamm-Bamm to Papa Smurf, had to invent a new type of speech for Scooby. "I had to come up with what I call 'growl talk,'" he said. "The words were there. Joe [Barbera] liked things starting with R's, for the dogs especially. He got that from watching Soupy Sales in the early days." (Famous quote: Rooby-Rooby Roo!)
- Norville "Shaggy" Rogers, Scooby's best friend, was based on Bob Denver's characterization of Maynard G. Krebs in Dobie Gillis. He was voiced by deejay Casey Kasem. (Famous quote: "Zoiks!")

- Velma Dinkley (voice: Nicole Jaffe), the brains of the outfit, was blind as a bat without her glasses. She also seemed to know every language on earth. (Famous quote, whenever she figured out a clue: "Jinkees!")
- Daphne Blake (voice: Heather North)was wealthy red-headed beauty who seemed to have no purpose on the show at all. Occasionally, she'd accidentally stumble on a clue. (Famous quote: "Oops!")
- Freddie Jones (voice: Frank Welker), the good-looking leader of the gang, always made Shaggy do the dangerous stuff. (Famous quote: "We'll split up. Velma, you go with Scooby and Shaggy, and I'll go with Daphne.") Hmmm . . . maybe Daphne did have a purpose after all.

The Numbers

The show was an instant success. It took over Saturday mornings in the 1970s and eventually set a still-unbroken record as the longest-running continuously produced children's animated show. Eighteen years passed before television was without some new incarnation of *Scooby-Doo*. In all, there were more than 10 different series with the name "Scooby-Doo" in them. One, *A Pup Named Scooby-Doo* (1990), included 10 other dogs, all related to Scooby. The most famous was Scooby's nephew, Scrappy-Doo. According to a recent poll on the Internet, Scrappy was the most annoying cartoon character of all time.

For more cartoon dogs, turn to page 192.

It's a Howl

*Can you match each dog-titled ditty with
its most-famous singer or band?*

1. "Black Dog"

2. "Dirty Old Egg-Suckin' Dog"

3. "Hound Dog"

4. "The Dog Song"

5. "Shoot the Dog"

6. "Call Me a Dog"

7. "Dog Eat Dog"

8. "Atomic Dog"

9. "Doggy Dogg World"

10. "(How Much Is) That
    Doggy in the Window?"

A. Elvis Presley

B. George Clinton

C. Temple of the Dog

D. Patti Page

E. Johnny Cash

F. Led Zeppelin

G. Nellie McKay

H. Snoop Dogg

I. Weird Al Yankovic

J. George Michael

For answers, turn to page 225.

The Nose Knows

Scientists are just discovering that certain diseases and medical conditions can be detected by smell, and many of those researchers are using dogs to sniff them out.

Cancer: The Proof's in the Pee

It's not easy finding scientific proof that dogs can smell cancer because no one knows exactly what odor the dogs are identifying. But some trainers and scientists have come up with methods to teach dogs how to sniff out the disease.

In 2004, at a hospital in Buckinghamshire, England, scientist Carolyn Willis set out rows of urine samples from people with and without bladder cancer and, with the help of a dog trainer, rewarded six different dogs whenever they lay down in front of the urine from a cancer patient. Some of the dogs did better than others, but all were able to identify the samples from patients who had bladder cancer. The dogs seemed to be making a mistake when all six chose one sample that had been included as a ringer—it was from a supposedly healthy patient. That patient's doctor was alarmed after the demonstration and did further tests. He discovered a previously undiagnosed kidney tumor. The dogs had been right all along!

Diabetes: The Blood Hound

Dogs can be trained to sniff out diabetes, too. Cody, a golden retriever from Oakland, California, keeps Devin Grayson from the danger of hypoglycemia—low blood sugar—that is a constant threat for people with type 1 (insulin-dependent) diabetes. Although diabetics often use glucose monitors to detect drops in blood sugar, these devices don't keep track of a patient's blood sugar levels all the time. Cody can sniff out drops in Grayson's blood sugar at any time of day or night, even when she's asleep. He licks her until she gets up and won't stop until she stabilizes her blood sugar.

Cody was trained at Dogs 4 Diabetics, a California non-profit center founded by Mark Ruefenacht. Since 2004, the group has been taking in dogs that don't quite make it as guide dogs for the blind and training them to identify hypoglycemia by smell. The dogs play a game of "find the shirt" that has come from a person in a hypoglycemic episode: several trainers carry various shirts, and the dog

that sniffs out the hypoglycemic one wins . . . and gets a treat. A diabetic himself, Ruefenacht depends on Armstrong, a

Labrador retriever who travels with him and uses his nose to help keep his owner healthy.

Epilepsy: There's a Smell for That?

Seizures also give off a scent, but because no one has any idea how to duplicate the smell, no one has officially trained a dog to detect an oncoming seizure. Instead, training organizations concentrate on obedience training and developing a deep emotional bond between dog and owner. In many cases, that bond is enough to get the dogs to respond and alert their owners to oncoming seizures. Sometimes, the dogs notice a seizure 20 to 45 minutes before it actually occurs. They may bark, yelp, jump, or paw to give the warning so the owner has time to get to a safe place or position before losing consciousness.

Cooper, the golden retriever companion of Katie Kemper of Cincinnati, Ohio, not only insists that his owner sit and stay when he senses a seizure is coming on, he also lies on top of her to protect her from thrashing too much and injuring herself. Cooper was trained at Amazing Tails, a Pennsylvania-based service training facility. The trainers there got Cooper from a local shelter, where he was considered too energetic and hyperactive to be adopted. They taught him to help Kemper when she was weak and disoriented after a seizure by letting her lean on him while she walks, opening doors, and getting outside help if she needs it.

Fido Follies

*Dogs may be man's best friend, but they
don't always make good decisions.*

Stinky

What he did: In December 2000, Stinky and his master,
Kelly Russell, were hunting near their New Zealand home.
Russell set down his rifle for a moment, and Stinky
jumped on it. The gun went off, hitting Russell in the
foot. At the hospital, doctors were unable to save Russell's
foot, and it had to be
amputated. He was also
fined $500 for hunting
illegally in an exotic
forest.

Jake

What he did: The
Dodson family of
Norman, Oklahoma,
went out one evening
and left Jake in the
same place they always
left him: the utility

room. They returned hours later to find a smoking pile of rubble where their home used to be. Jake had flipped the gas line switch, filling the room with natural gas, and when the hot water heater kicked on, the gas exploded. Although the house was destroyed, Jake was hurled clear of the explosion and escaped unharmed.

Bear

What he did: Glen Shaw, a trash collector in New Hampshire, occasionally brought his dog Bear along on his route. Usually, there was no trouble. But on December 20, 2001, Shaw got out of his 10-wheeled compactor truck to load some garbage into the back, and Bear somehow released the hand brake. As the truck began to roll downhill, Shaw ran after it, but it was no use. The runaway truck plunged into the Souhegan River, and Shaw plunged in behind it to rescue his dog. Bear survived, but it took a hazardous waste crew more than two hours to clean up the mess.

To read about "good" dogs, turn to pages 6 and 217.

* * *

"Dogs are our link to paradise. They don't know evil or jealousy or discontent. To sit with a dog on a hillside on a glorious afternoon is to be back in Eden, where doing nothing wasn't boring—it was peace."

—Milan Kundera

Bow-wow Wow!

From plush dog beds to luxurious carriers to monogrammed collars, these three designers have all gone to the dogs.

Gucci

This Italian design house was the first to jump on the luxury dog-product bandwagon. Back in 1997, designer Tom Ford—the man credited with turning Gucci into a modern fashion powerhouse—was running the business. One of Ford's many innovations for the company was to sell fancy dog collars and leashes to the wealthy who pampered their pooches. Ten years later, Gucci's dog line has expanded to include these luxury items:

- Mattresses. Price: $420.
- Carriers (with washable interiors). Price: $2,250.
- Quilted dog coats (some with wool trim). Price: $270.
- Caps. Price: $86.

(All of the Gucci products are adorned with the label's signature "G," of course.)

Louis Vuitton

Louis Vuitton was the second major design house to see dollar signs in dogs, with a monogrammed dog collar ($250) and leash ($245). (There are more expensive versions made with goat leather and cow hide.) Vuitton, famous for high-end pocketbooks and luggage, also offers two dog carriers: one retails for $1,620, the other for $1,770.

Burberry

This British design house has a line of canine outerwear. (Hey, it gets chilly in London!)

- The cotton trench coat looks a lot like something Sherlock Holmes would wear and is dry-clean only. Price: $225.
- The parka comes with a detachable hood (also dry-clean only). Price: $170.
- Burberry's dog sweater is made of merino wool and is washing-machine friendly. Price: $215.

Burberry also offers a dog bowl ($75), a dog bed ($395), and a dog carrier ($950), which all sport the signature Burberry plaid. (Their dog leash is plaid-less but has brass hardware . . . and costs a cool $185.)

Here Comes Rin Tin Tin!

From the 1920s to the 1950s, one Hollywood
canine stood paw and tail above the rest.

From Shellshock to Show Biz

The year was 1918, and U.S. Army Corporal Lee Duncan was stationed in Lorraine, France. He and his battalion came upon a bombed dog kennel and found a starving mother dog and her five German shepherd puppies. The soldiers rescued the animals, and Duncan took two of the puppies as his own. He named them Rin Tin Tin and Nannette after a pair of French puppets local children had given his unit for good luck. When the war ended, Duncan took the dogs back to the United States. The journey took a toll on Nannette, and she died soon after they arrived. But Rin Tin Tin (or Rinty, as Duncan called him) settled easily into a new life in Los Angeles.

Soon Duncan had taught Rinty some tricks, and the pooch was quick to catch on. One of his most impressive stunts was the high jump: 11 feet, 9 inches. Duncan took Rinty to various dog shows in Southern California, and at one in L.A. in 1922, a cameraman named Charles Jones was in the audience. Jones was so impressed by Rinty's skills, demeanor, and looks (the dog had handsome dark fur) that he paid Duncan $350 to let him film the canine.

That film eventually made it to producers at Warner Bros. Studios, and Rinty's Hollywood career began.

A Dog's Life

When Rinty arrived at the studio, Warner Bros. was struggling financially and on the verge of bankruptcy, but the heroic dog saved the day. His first film was *The Man from Hell's River* in 1922, and it was a hit. Ultimately, Rin Tin Tin starred in 26 movies for Warner Bros. He also had his own radio show—*The Wonder Dog*—in the 1930s. All this work made Rinty a superstar. By 1926, he earned up to $6,000 and received 10,000 fan letters each week. Hollywood legend claims that Rinty listened to classical music and even had his own personal chef, who prepared him a sirloin steak lunch every day.

Rin Tin Tin died in 1932 at home in Los Angeles, in the arms of one of Duncan's Hollywood friends—actress Jean Harlow. He was buried in France.

Happy Tails

After the original Rin Tin Tin had passed on, his descendants followed him into Hollywood careers. Two of Rinty's grandsons—named Rin Tin Tin II and IV—starred in a CBS TV show, *The Adventures of Rin Tin Tin* (1954–59). (Previously, the show had been broadcast on the radio.) The dogs, both trained by Duncan, alternated as the show's lead, a gutsy dog who was rescued by cavalry soldiers after most of his human family was killed in a Wild

West wagon train raid. The only human survivor: an orphan named Rusty, who became Rin Tin Tin's pal.

Rin Tin Tin and Rusty had many adventures together. They dodged the straight-laced curmudgeon-with-a-heart Colonel Barker (who commanded the cavalry unit), saved the soldiers from an ambush, and confronted mountain lions, bears, and wild horses.

Long Live Rinty!

Not wanting his famous dog's legacy to die out completely, Duncan enlisted German shepherd breeder, Jannettia Propps and her Texas kennel to carry on the original Rin Tin Tin's bloodline by breeding his descendants. Propps started breeding Rin Tin Tins in 1957, and by 2007, there had been a total of 10 Rin Tin Tins. All were descended from Duncan's original dog, making Rinty one of the longest continuous German shepherd bloodlines in the world. Lee Duncan died in 1960 and Jannettia Propps in 1988, but the Texas kennel, called Bodyguard Kennel, continues to breed the dogs under the watchful eye of Propps' granddaughter Daphne Hereford.

* * *

"The greatest pleasure of a dog is that you may make a fool of yourself with him, and not only will he not scold you, but he will make a fool of himself too."

—*Samuel Butler*

Love Story

How much do you love your dog?

1 percent of dog owners . . . throw their pooches birthday parties.

33 percent of dog owners . . . talk to their dogs on the phone.

55 percent of dog owners . . . buy their dogs Christmas gifts.

58 percent of dog owners . . . include their pets in family portraits.

60 percent of dog owners . . . have a coat, sweater, or raincoat to keep their furry friends warm and dry.

70 percent of dog owners . . . sign their pet's name to holiday and greeting cards.

87 percent of dog owners . . . curl up with their pooch to watch TV.

88 percent of dog owners . . . give their pets treats daily.

Ask the Experts

*Dogs certainly do lots of peculiar things. To find out why,
we asked the folks at the American Society for the Prevention
of Cruelty to Animals. Here's what they said.*

Why do dogs sniff each other?

Dogs have such a sensitive sense of smell that sniffing is
the best way for them to get to know each other. When
two dogs meet, they sniff each other's rear ends to gather
information on gender, fear, submission, and reproductive
status. When a dog sniffs you, he's learning your unique
odor and gauging your emotional state.

Why do dogs circle before settling down for a nap?

Before dogs were domesticated and kept as pets in the
house, dogs had to tramp down grass to create a warm, safe
bed for the night. Circling their sleeping space, even in a
comfortable room in the house, is probably a throwback to
that instinct.

Why do dogs mark fire hydrants?

A male dog will mark on any vertical object available.
It's his way of adding his scent to the neighborhood;
dogs who come along later can gather information on all

the dogs in a given area by smelling the different scents. Male dogs are much more likely to mark than females, although female dogs do mark when they're in heat, when the pheromone-laced urine they leave behind is meant to attract a mate.

Why is my dog's nose always wet?

The moisture on a dog's nose helps to capture and dissolve molecules of scent. It's also a good—although not always precise—indicator of your dog's general health. A dry nose can be a sign of illness.

Why does my dog drag his butt along the ground?

This is usually a sign that a dog's anal sacs (which they use to mark their territory) have become impacted and are causing the dog discomfort. The sacs need to be emptied or they can get infected. With a little practice, the dog's owner can easily empty the sacs, but if that makes you queasy, call the vet.

Why do dogs tremble?

When a dog trembles, he's usually communicating sub-mission. Submissive dogs also roll onto their backs, paw the ground, duck a friendly pat, urinate nervously, or lower their bodies to a slouching position.

Why do dogs mount other dogs . . . and people's legs?

The most common reason for a mature dog to mount is for sexual positioning. But even puppies mount when they play. If a dog mounts a human, it's usually a show of dominance. This behavior should be discouraged with a sharp "no."

* * *

Mickey's Best Friend

A few random facts about Mickey Mouse's canine companion, Pluto:

- He made his film debut in 1930 as an unnamed bloodhound in the Disney short *The Chain Gang*.
- Next, he appeared in *The Picnic* as Minnie Mouse's dog Rover.
- Finally, in 1931's *The Moose Hunt*, he was christened Pluto (named for the recently discovered dwarf planet) and became Mickey's pal.

Happy Bark Mitzvah

*How do you know when your puppy becomes
a dog? When it's time for his Bark Mitzvah!*

The Hebrew term "Bar Mitzvah" means "son of the
commandment." It's a religious initiation ceremony
for a Jewish boy to celebrate his 13th birthday, mark his
coming of age as a member of his community, and emphasize the beginning of his religious responsibilities. (A Bat
Mitzvah is the ceremony for girls.) Bar and Bat Mitzvahs
are often social events with lavish receptions that feature
catered dinners, hired entertainment, and partying into
the wee hours. Yet even such elaborate occasions have
nothing on a Bark Mitzvah bash for Rover.

Party Animals

During the past decade, some devoted Jewish dog owners
began thinking that their canine friends deserved a rite of
passage too, but nailing down the age at which a puppy
becomes a dog is hard. Some owners stick to the human
milestone of 13 years. Celebrity Joan Rivers gave her dog
Spike a Bark Mitzvah for his 13th birthday that would
include "a gala celebration with lots of four-legged friends
and their celebrity owners." Others throw a party for a dog
who is 13 in "doggy years." (Since the accepted conversion

is seven dog years for every human year, this translates to a Bark Mitzvah for a dog just under two years of age.) And still others choose a more arbitrary time, holding Bark Mitzvahs when their beloved pet leaves puppyhood and becomes a "responsible" dog. Steven and Kathleen Estrella threw their Cardigan Welsh corgi Clara Belle a Bark Mitzvah in the hope that she would grow up well and obey five doggy commandments, including "thou shalt not bark at 2 a.m."

Like the celebrations of their human counterparts, some Bark Mitzvahs are spiritually oriented and might include a blessing for the dog and those attending the festivities and maybe a traditional prayer. Others, of course, are just a great excuse to be a party animal. Either way, Bark Mitzvahs usually have all the lavish trimmings of the real deal. They include printed invitations, Hebrew and Yiddish folk music, gift registries, dog toys shaped like menorahs, or maybe a game called "ice hockey," where the top dog and his guests chase a liver snack frozen in a block of ice across the floor.

Fashion and Food

Image is everything, so traditional religious accessories, though not de rigueur, are usually encouraged. At some Bark Mitzvahs, the animals wear yarmulkes (Jewish skull caps); at others, the dogs don prayer shawls. One Jack Russell terrier from Illinois wore a tuxedo for his party. And like the human parents of a Bar Mitzvah boy, the beaming parents of the Bark Mitzvah dog get a congratulatory "muzzle tov" from their human guests.

Of course, any celebration needs refreshments. Doggy treats arrive in cake and cookie form, sometimes sporting Jewish symbols like a Star of David, sometimes decorated with blue and white frosting to represent the colors on the Israeli flag. And the treats served at Bark Mitzvahs are often kosher.

Too Much Puppy Love?

Some rabbis object to Bark Mitzvahs. New York rabbi Avi Shafran was quoted in the *Jewish Daily Forward* newspaper as saying, "Once you leave the bounds of the human race, it becomes nonsensical to talk about Jewishness." The rabbi does note, however, that "the Talmud says that when people come home they have to feed their animals before they feed themselves. I feed my tropical fish before I eat dinner each night."

Other religious leaders, though, respect their congregations' desires to treat their dog children like human children. Rabbi Neil Comess-Daniels of Beth Shir Shalom, a Reform temple in California, holds group Bark Mitzvahs in the synagogue's parking lot. His ceremonies are open to all pets, and the congregation sings a celebratory animal prayer that includes the lines "May our God protect and defend you. May God always shield you from fleas." Although the Bark Mitzvah is a fun event that allows his congregation to show its sense of humor, Rabbi Comess-Daniels told the *Forward* that Bark Mitzvahs also have a serious side: "People are bringing their pets into the spiritual parts of their lives and expressing it in a Jewish, communal way."

Remarkable Reunions

Take a look at the mishaps and misadventures of some truly amazing dogs who just wanted to go home.

Cinnamon: Afghani Refugee

In October 2005, Lt. Cmdr. Mark Feffer met a three-month-old beige mutt while he was stationed in Afghanistan. He called the dog Cinnamon, and she became well known (and well liked) among the soldiers in his unit. Six months later, when Feffer's tour in Afghanistan was over, he made arrangements to take Cinnamon home with him to Cape St. Claire, Maryland. Because he wasn't a military dog handler, Feffer wasn't allowed to transport Cinnamon himself. But he found a civilian who was willing to check Cinnamon as baggage at the Manas International Airport in Afghanistan. At first, all seemed fine, but when the civilian deplaned in New York, Feffer learned that Cinnamon hadn't been put on the plane after all. She'd been left with the baggage handler in Afghanistan, who'd mistakenly given the dog to someone else at the airport.

Stateside, Feffer's sister took over Cinnamon's bungled journey. She contacted the World Society for the Protection of Animals, figuring that even if she couldn't get Cinnamon to the United States, she wanted to know the dog was in good hands. The World Society found the dog and her new owner, and initially, the two were happy together. But within a month, the new owner blamed Cinnamon for killing his chickens and wanted to get rid of her. Feffer was happy to oblige. Cinnamon went back to the Manas airport and was put in the custody of the person in charge of military airport security. He arranged for her to be escorted to New York, where Feffer picked her up. This time, there were no snags. Forty-four days, 7,000 miles, and several dead chickens later, Cinnamon arrived at her new home in Maryland, where she now hunts for squirrels in the backyard, relaxes in front of the air-conditioning vents, and has retired from world travel.

Emma: On the Run

In June 2005, Emma, a black bichon frise/Shih Tzu, mix was traveling with her family from Edmonton, Canada, to a family reunion in Winnipeg. Along a stretch of the Trans-Canada Highway

in Saskatchewan, the family was involved in a serious car accident: their SUV rolled three times and landed on the passenger side. Luckily, the family and Emma were all buckled in. Emma was in her pet carrier, which was secured to the seat, but the carrier was ejected from the car and its door opened, giving an uninjured but frightened Emma the opportunity to run for it.

The family suffered only minor injuries, but they were all rushed to the emergency room, leaving their dog behind. Rescuers searched for Emma but found no sign of her so the family had to return to Edmonton empty-handed, but the dog's story wasn't over.

Several days after the accident, a farmer discovered a dehydrated, hungry, scruffy, and very frightened Emma in a canola field about a half-mile from the accident site. The farmer had heard about the accident and the missing dog, and he tried to catch her. He even brought out his trapping dog, but Emma evaded capture. Finally, one afternoon, he spied the little black dog in the field. The farmer chased Emma until he got close enough to throw a shirt over her. At last, the pooch was safe. Two weeks after the accident, Emma was reunited with her family.

Bobby: Dog-Gone

Eighty-year-old Lillian Brown of Apache Junction, Arizona, adored her two-year-old terrier-beagle mix, Bobby. She had adopted him from a shelter soon after her husband of 48 years had died. Bobby lifted the elderly woman's spirits and became an important part of her life. Lillian's elderly neighbor, Cheryll, also took a liking to Bobby and even offered Lillian money for him. Lillian didn't want to sell her dog, but she was willing to let Bobby visit Cheryll at her house.

The situation remained innocent enough until Cheryll, who wintered in Arizona and lived the rest of the year in Indiana, left for home. That day, while Lillian was out running errands, Bobby disappeared. A neighborhood search proved fruitless, and Lillian, after spending many nights on her porch awaiting her pet's return, finally turned to the local newspaper for help. One reporter-turned-sleuth sensed foul play and investigated the dog's disappearance.

Suspicious of Cheryll, the reporter sent letters to many of the woman's Indiana neighbors asking if they had seen Bobby. One of them had. The police stepped in and charged Cheryll with theft. Bobby went home to Lillian two months after he was dognapped.

For more reunions, turn to page 184.

Madison Avenue Mutts

From beer to burritos, we know what these pups are selling.

Nipper, the RCA Dog

Nipper, a fox terrier, was born in England in 1884 and got his name because he liked to bite visitors on their legs. His original owner was Mark Barroud, brother of English painter Francis Barroud. When Mark died, Francis inherited the dog. According to legend, when a recording of Mark's voice was played at his funeral, Nipper recognized it and stood on Mark's coffin, looking into the horn of the phonograph. Francis Barroud later painted the scene in a work titled *His Master's Voice*. Around 1900, the Victor Talking Machine Company started using the painting as its logo. Then, in 1928, Nipper (minus the coffin) became the symbol of the Radio Corporation of America when Victor's American rights were sold to RCA.

Spuds McKenzie

"Some guy in our Chicago agency drew a rough sketch of a dog called the Party Animal, for a Bud Light poster," Anheuser-Busch's marketing director told *Sports Illustrated*. "So we had to find a real dog that looked like this drawing." The company picked Honey Tree Evil Eye, a female English bull terrier from Illinois. The poster was supposed to be distributed only to college students, but the beer company's spokesdog was such a hit that the ads started showing up everywhere. After Spuds made her TV debut during the 1987 Super Bowl, Bud Light sales shot up 20 percent. Spuds retired amid controversy some time later when the group Mothers Against Drunk Driving accused Anheuser-Busch of using the dog to encourage underage drinking. Honey Tree returned home to Illinois, where she lived until her death in 1993. She was 10 years old.

The Taco Bell Chihuahua

The most famous fast-food character of the 1990s was invented by chance when two advertising executives, Chuck Bennett and Clay Williams, were eating lunch at the Tortilla Grill in Venice, California. "We saw a little Chihuahua run by that appeared to be on a mission," Bennett says. "We both looked at each other and said, 'That would be funny.'" The men went on to make Gidget—the model Chihuahua used in the ads—an international superstar. The dog spawned toys, bobble-heads, and a renewed interest in the Chihuahua breed. (A respected canine thespian in her own right, Gidget also starred in other projects, most notably as Bruiser's mother in the 2003 film *Legally Blonde 2: Red, White, and Blonde*.)

McGruff the Crime Dog

In the late 1970s, the Ad Council—the organization responsible for producing most public-service announcements—made a deal with the U.S. Justice Department to create an ad campaign to discourage crime. Their first task: invent a spokes-character to deliver the message in commercials. Adman Jack Keil began riding with the New York police to get ideas. He remembers:

We weren't getting anywhere. Then came a day I was flying home from the West Coast. I was trying to think of a slogan—*crunch crime, stomp on crime*. And I was thinking of animal symbols—*growling at crime, roaring at crime*. But which animal? The designated critter had to be trustworthy, honorable, and brave. Then I thought, you can't crunch crime or defeat it altogether, but you can snap at it, nibble at it—*take a bite out of crime*. And the animal that takes a bite is a dog.

A bloodhound was the natural choice for a crime fighter, and the campaign (dog included) debuted in 1980. But Keil still needed a name for his watchdog, so the Ad Council sponsored a nationwide contest to name the dog. Entries included Shure-lock Bones, Sarg-dog, J. Edgar Dog, and Keystone Kop Dog. The winner was submitted by a police officer from New Orleans—McGruff. In the ads, Keil supplies the dog's voice. When he retires, Steve Parker, a sheriff's deputy from Indiana, will take over.

Fine Art Fidos

Dogs have provided inspiration to many famous painters and photographers. See how much you know about famous dog art, the artists who create it, and the pets who love them.

1. In 2005, an art collector paid $590,400 for two of a series of nine dog-themed paintings by Cassius Marcellus Coolidge. By what name are the paintings (more often found hanging on a frat house wall than in an art gallery) collectively known?

2. What Pop artist, best known for his portraits of soup cans, became a zealous dog lover after acquiring a dachshund named Archie?

3. What diminutive post-Impressionist painter (and frequent customer of the La Souris restaurant in France), drew a famous sketch of the restaurant's owner and her dog, entitled *Bouboule: Mme. Palmyre's Bulldog*?

4. After receiving a dog from one of his patrons, Dutch painter Hieronymus Bosch became so enamored with the pet that he put him in Eden in which of his most *Delight*-ful (and sinful) creations?

5. What Cubist and his dog were the subjects of David Duncan's book of photographs, chronicling the special relationship between artist and pet? (The two even passed away within a week of each other.)

6. What Mexican artist, who married a famous Mexican muralist and was best known for her colorful self-portraits, collected a menagerie of exotic animals, including a half dozen Xoloitzcuintles (a larger, hairless, and bark-less Chihuahua cousin)?

7. What American painter of *Boy and Dog in a Johnnypump*, initially known for his graffiti art and as a friend and collaborator of Andy Warhol, died of a drug overdose in 1988 at the age of 28?

8. In the painting *The Marriage of Giovanni Arnolfini and Giovanna Cenami* by 15th-century Dutchman Jan Van Eyck, what "faithful" characteristic is the griffon terrier at the couple's feet supposed to represent?

Answers on page 226.

Sheriff's Top Dog

This little police dog is making a big name for herself.

These days, many police officers would be lost without their K-9 units. The dogs sniff out drugs, track down bad guys, find lost hikers, and otherwise assist their human colleagues in the daily goings-on of police departments around the world. The animals are usually fierce protectors—German shepherds, bloodhounds, and other hefty breeds are the norm. But the sheriff's office in Munson Township, Ohio, has a more dainty canine crime fighter.

World's Smallest Police Dog?

There aren't any official statistics, but Midge, a nearly two-year-old Chihuahua/rat terrier mix, is likely the world's smallest police dog. She weighs just seven pounds and belongs to the Munson Township sheriff, Dan McClelland, who adopted her as a puppy. Midge was a runt, weighing two pounds when he brought her home. But McClelland saw potential in the tiny dog: she was a curious sniffer, always nosing around. He also saw the limitations of his canine force, which at the time consisted of five German shepherds and a Lab. His big dogs had trouble maneuvering in tight spaces—searching a car interior

100

for drugs, for example. And in some places, suspects whose cars K-9 units had rummaged through were suing police departments for damages. McClelland wondered if a smaller dog wouldn't be helpful.

So he decided to experiment with Midge. He trained her himself, teaching her to find marijuana when she was just three months old. McClelland says, "There's no reason why a small dog can't be as effective as a big dog."

Just a Softie

She's also cute and is able to melt the hearts of even the most fearsome foes. Brutus, a 125-pound drug-sniffing German shepherd, doesn't get along with many of the other dogs in McClelland's K-9 unit. In fact, most of the big dogs, all males, fight for dominance when they're together. But they love Midge. From the time she was just a puppy, Brutus befriended her, and today, the two are pals. They play together, and Brutus even lets Midge nap on his stomach. She's also a beloved participant in the county jail's meet-and-greet canine program. As a reward for good behavior, inmates can spend time with the sheriff's police dogs, and Midge is an often-requested favorite. The inmates play with her—she likes to nibble on their toes—and open up about missing their own dogs at home. For Midge, the activity is just another part of her training; it's a great way for her to learn social skills.

By far, though, Midge's best friend is McClelland himself. She spends a lot of time dozing on his lap and even has her own goggles for when the two go on motorcycle rides together. The officer also likes to show her off at schools around the county, where Midge teaches kids one of McClelland's favorite truisms: "Even when you're small, if you take a stand, you can make a difference."

Not Just for Chihuahuas Anymore

Midge may be the smallest, but she isn't the only little dog helping out law enforcement. At the Canadian border, U.S. Customs officers use beagles to search luggage for bombs. And various trainers around the country specifically work with smaller dogs—those who weigh 40 pounds or less—and prepare them for jobs in law enforcement. According to Dave Blosser, one of those trainers, "Size-wise, endurance-wise, they last longer."

* * *

"No one appreciates the very special genius of your conversation as the dog does."

—*Christopher Morley*

Dog Tales

*Dogs show up in folklore from around the world—as
fearsome protectors, terrifying monsters, and steadfast pets. Here
are some of the canine characters from those mythologies.*

Cu Sith

This shaggy green hound appeared in Celtic mythology,
where he roamed the Scottish Highlands. He was about
the size of a cow and was a part of the fairy realm. Every
night, just after dusk, he barked three times so loudly that
ships in the ocean could hear him. The Celts took this as
a sign that they ought to lock up their women: Cu Sith
(pronounced "coo shee") would abduct any womenfolk
caught unawares and use them to supply milk for fairy
children.

Quick fact: Most canines in Celtic myth are black or
brown, so Cu Sith's green fur set him apart from other legendary Celtic dogs. This is why he was thought to be part
of the fairy world—Celtic fairies are often green.

Cerberus

This three-headed "Hound of Hades" guarded the Greek
underworld and was the offspring of Echidna and Typhon,
two serpentine beasts that also produced the Chimera (a

creature made up of several animals) and Hydra (a sea serpent with many heads). Cerberus was most famously featured in the story of the Greek hero Hercules, who had fallen from grace for killing his wife and children and had to participate in 12 tasks to save his soul. Capturing Cerberus and delivering him to the Mycenaean king Eurystheus was Hercules' final task. It was no easy feat; Cerberus wasn't supposed to leave the Underworld, and the living weren't supposed to go into it. The Underworld's rulers, Hades and Persephone, finally agreed to let him take Cerberus as long as he didn't hurt the dog. Hercules managed to wrestle the hound into submission and took him aboveground. After showing Cerberus to Eurystheus (who was so frightened that he jumped into a storage jar), Hercules returned the dog unharmed to the Underworld.

Quick fact: In some legends, Cerberus sports as many as 100 heads, but three is the most common number.

Argos

Argos may be the most loyal dog in legend. In the epic Greek poem *The Odyssey*, Homer chronicles the trials and tribulations of Argos' owner—the hero Odysseus—as he made his way home from the Trojan War. Odysseus was gone for about 20 years (traveling to the war, fighting it, and then trying to get home). He finally arrived home in his kingdom of Ithaca, dressed as a beggar to spy on his wife Penelope and any men who wanted to court her. He needn't have worried, though. Penelope kept the suitors at bay, telling them she would marry only the man who could bend a bow made by her husband. None succeeded.

When Odysseus arrived in Ithaca, though, Argos immediately recognized his master. And having waited so long to see Odysseus again, the faithful (and incredibly old) Argos finally died with just a single whimper.

Quick fact: In homage to Odysseus' long journey, NASA named a space mission after him, using his Roman name, Ulysses. The *Ulysses* spacecraft launched in 1990 and spent 12 years collecting data about the sun.

For more mythological dogs, turn to page 207.

* * *

Doggy Lingo

In English, dogs go "Bow-wow!" But they can also speak other languages:

Swedish: Voff voff!
Hebrew: Hav Hav!
Chinese: Wang-wang!
Japanese: Won-won!
Swahili: Hu Hu Hu Huuu!

Three Dog Bakery

Dogs in the United States, Canada, and Japan have fallen head over paws for these treats.

Thank Gracie

Inspiration comes from many places. In the case of Kansas City friends Dan Dye and Mark Beckloff, it came in the form of a Great Dane named Gracie. In 1989, Dye found Gracie in a litter of puppies. She was small, slower than the rest, deaf, blind in one eye, and easily frightened. But Dye loved her right away and brought her home. Gracie had a fantastic personality; she was loving and smart. But physically, she was delicate. In an effort to boost her health, Dye started cooking. He made her all kinds of treats and foods using healthy, natural ingredients that he could eat himself: peanut butter, vegetables, wheat, fruits, and honey. Gracie loved the eats, and, as Dye found out, so did (and his friend Mark Beckloff's) other dogs: Dottie (a Dalmatian) and Sarah Jean the Biscuit Queen (a black Lab mix).

A Business Is Born

Armed with a 59-cent biscuit cutter, Dye and Beckloff decided to start a business to sell their treats. They named it the Three Dog Bakery (after Gracie, Dottie, and Sarah

Jean) and set up shop in Kansas City. The response from local customers was tremendous: dogs loved the formulas, and owners loved knowing that they were feeding their pooches healthy snacks.

Word quickly spread beyond Kansas City, and the guys started selling their snacks in Neiman Marcus stores and national pet supply chains. Three Dog Bakery also launched its own DOGalog—a shop-at-home service for pampered puppy owners who wanted to order gourmet treats by mail.

Vanilla Woofer, Anyone?

Today, there are more than 40 Three Dog Bakery franchises in the United States, two in Canada, and 10 in Japan. Dye and Beckloff are hoping to expand to Western Europe soon, and predict that by 2010, there will be more than 130 Three Dog Bakeries worldwide.

The bakery's success, of course, is in the products. Some of the playfully named items include Ruffles (cakelike cookies rolled in carob, peanut crumbles, and coconut flakes), Vanilla Woofers (vanilla cookies), and Jump 'n Sit Bits (nuggets made with oatmeal, peanut butter, apples, cheese, and carob). They also offer dog food and specialty treats (like the whole wheat and peanut butter dino bone, on which they'll write a message to your pooch in carob syrup). All the goodies are displayed in a temperature-controlled glass display case, just like in a traditional bakery.

Dye and Beckloff also believe that their stores should be a gathering place for dogs and their "leash-slaves." So Three Dog Bakeries routinely host dog events, including an Easter Begg Hunt for Dogs and Growl-oween Costume Parades. In 2007, they added another celebration, the "World's Largest Dog Party" on Cinco de Mayo.

And the guys remain dedicated to helping dogs in need. Gracie died in 1999, but a foundation they set up in her name (aptly called the Gracie Foundation) acts as a sort of Red Cross for dogs in distress. The foundation works with a number of other groups around the United States to provide response and supplies to pets in emergency situations, with a focus on rescuing dogs.

* * *

The Great Dog Lover

The Roman historian Plutarch wrote that Alexander the Great had a dog named Peritas, whom he raised from puppyhood. After Peritas died, Alexander named a city for him. (Alexander also named a city for his horse, Bucephalas.)

From Tragedy
to Triumph

*In 2006, a blue-eyed Siberian husky named Triumph became
the first dog to receive permanent prosthetic legs.*

An Incredible Journey

In late 2002, a Good Samaritan found Triumph by the side
of a road in Turkey. The dog was in bad shape: both of her
back legs were missing, and she was close to death. She
was taken to an animal shelter, where volunteers nursed
her back to health. As she recovered, they tried to find
her a home. With no immediate takers, two shelter work-
ers contacted a local Turkish newspaper for publicity. After
that, Triumph's story hit the Internet, where Marion
Moeller of Nashville, Tennessee, read about her. Moeller
worked with abused dogs, and she knew she could help
Triumph.

Bringing the dog to the United States was expensive,
but Moeller managed to raise the money. She also contacted a man who made prosthetic limbs for animals and
secured the dog a set of artificial legs. After Triumph
arrived in the United States in 2003, she got the new legs,
and with some physical therapy and rehabilitation, she
was running and playing in no time.

Making Medical History

But Moeller figured, why stop at temporary limbs? She took Triumph to Denver to see veterinarian Robert Taylor, who was researching a surgery that would give amputee dogs permanent artificial legs. Moeller says Triumph was an excellent candidate for the surgery because "her injury was traumatic [rather than the result of disease] and her temperament was clearly one of a survivor . . . she is very gentle and never complained, but cooperated."

Between August 2005 and December 2006, Triumph made seven trips to Denver for three surgeries and multiple checkups. Things didn't always go smoothly. An infection in the dog's left leg, a loosened implant that required replacement, a hairline leg fracture, and other complications arose, but Moeller nursed Triumph though each one: she helped Triumph walk by holding a bellyband that supported about half of the dog's body weight, and the rest of the time, Moeller carried Triumph or used a stroller. Finally, after a final surgery that outfitted Triumph with special rubber feet, her treatment was finished. Today, she's almost completely independent.

The results from Triumph's surgery and recovery had another benefit: they gave doctors and medical professionals encouragement that one day the procedure could be used to treat human patients.

"The Smile Bringer"

Triumph's recovery isn't the end of the story. She still has a job to do. Soon after the dog arrived in the United States, Moeller signed her up to be a therapy dog. Today, Triumph specializes in boosting the spirits of children and adults at hospitals, nursing homes, and schools. Because of the dog's own handicap, critically ill children especially feel a bond with her. Moeller says of the children's reaction to Triumph, "They want to touch her. She brings a lot of laughter wherever she goes to anybody she meets." As such, Moeller calls Triumph the "Smile Bringer." "I think she was born to do this," says Moeller. "It's her mission in life."

* * *

Going to the Chapel

Sculptor and artist Stephen Huneck from St. Johnsbury, Vermont, almost died a few years ago. He contracted a respiratory disease that put him in a coma. His doctors didn't have high hopes for his recovery. Two months later, when he finally woke up, Huneck had to relearn the simplest tasks . . . everything from walking to using a fork. And he credited his three dogs—Labs Artie and Molly and a golden retriever named Sally—with helping him recover. It was that devotion that inspired the Dog Chapel atop Dog Mountain on Huneck's property. He designed the chapel himself, modeling it after early 19th-century New England country chapels: it's white, has a tall steeple, and sports a sculpture of a Lab at the steeple's tip. Dogs and their owners are always welcome.

The Power of . . .

Next time you take your dog out to do his business, consider this.

The European Way

What if your house were powered by dog poop? That idea may sound unbelievable (and gross), but officials in eco-and-dog-friendly San Francisco don't think so. They hope to harness the methane contained in canine waste and use it to generate electricity.

The idea isn't new. In the 19th century, Louis Pasteur discussed the possibility of making methane from farmyard manure, and the process is relatively simple. When organic material decays, it yields useful by-products. Dog feces contains bacteria called methanogens, which use hydrogen to break down carbon dioxide during decay and produce methane gas as a by-product. To make electricity, one need only to toss dog droppings into a large tank where the bacteria can do its dirty work; the resulting methane gas is then trapped in airtight containers and can be piped into a gas stove, heater, or any other household appliance powered by natural gas.

The technology caught on in Europe during World War II, when fuel shortages in Germany led to the development of methane plants. Today, more than 600 farm-based methane digesters operate in Europe, primarily in Denmark and Sweden. Swedish plants produce enough methane to operate 2,300 buses.

The Poo Project

The method has not yet gained widespread popularity in the United States, even though 16 diary farms across the country already convert manure to methane. But just after the millennium, the folks in San Francisco began investigating the energy potential of dog waste. It makes sense, of course. The city's dog population is one of the highest in the country: about 120,000 dogs live in the city limits (that's higher than the number of resident children) and dog waste makes up almost 4 percent of San Francisco's garbage. Plus, San Franciscans are used to recycling. So city officials hope that eventually they can turn the 6,500 tons of dog waste produced in San Francisco every year into energy.

The project began officially in 2006, and it's an extension of another recycling program San Franciscans started more than a decade ago—collecting food scraps from homes and restaurants and turning them into

fertilizer for organic farms and vineyards. (Today, 300 tons of food scraps are collected every day in San Francisco from thousands of restaurants and homes.) Norcal Waste, a sanitation company that collects the city's trash, uses biodegradable bags and dog-waste collection carts to pick up the poop every few days from the city's busiest dog parks. The program isn't yet widespread and it's still experimental, but it seems to be picking up speed and shows great promise for the future of Bay Area energy. Says Robert Reed, who works for Norcal, "Scraping dog poop off your shoe, now that's something most people have been frustrated with for a long time. Now we have an opportunity to turn this nuisance into something positive."

The Stats

Around the United States, energy costs are on the rise, so the San Francisco program seems to be coming at a perfect time for Americans and their dogs. Forty percent of U.S. households include at least one dog—that's more than 74 million dogs nationwide. And as more people, especially in cities, bring pooches into their homes, the dog waste problem keeps growing. Take a look at some of the statistics:

- In the United States, dogs produce more than 5,000 tons of waste daily. That would cover 800 football fields, one foot deep in poo.
- Before enacting a 1978 law that made it mandatory for New York City dog owners to clean up after their pets,

approximately 40 million pounds of dog droppings were left on the city's streets every year.

- A 1999 environmental survey found that 41 percent of dog owners rarely or never clean up after their dogs, and 44 percent say they would continue not to in spite of fines or neighbors' complaints.
- In 2001, the California Environmental Protection Agency estimated that owners in Los Angeles County walked their dogs without picking up after them 82,000 times per month.

* * *

Just Misunderstood

Pit bulls have a bad reputation, but it wasn't always that way. Early American settlers loved the breed, mostly because of the dogs' loyalty, stamina, and courage, and by the beginning of the 20th century, pit bulls (also called Yankee terriers) had become America's favorite dog. They showed up in the news (Stubby the pit bull was a decorated World War I hero) and in popular films (Petey was the lovable dog in *Our Gang*). And many American authors—including John Steinbeck, James Thurber, and Mark Twain—incorporated pit bulls into their writing. Pit bulls probably got their bad rep because the breed was often used in illegal dogfights in 19th-century England. But in reality, most of the dogs are actually quite stable and reliable, and many serve as therapy dogs in hospitals, nursing homes, and schools.

No Racer Left Behind

A greyhound can reach speeds of up to 45 mph in a matter of seconds, but at home, they are more likely to be called "45 mile an hour couch potatoes."

Greyhounds are the fastest dog breed in the world and one of the fastest animals, second only to the cheetah. Because of their speed, owners in the early 1900s turned them into race dogs. The first dog-racing track opened in 1919, and in 2007, there were 46 tracks operating in 15 states. When a greyhound's racing days are over, though (usually by the time he's five years old), he's ready to retire. Thousands of the dogs retire every year, and

rescue organizations like the Greyhound Pets of America, Inc. (GPA) have stepped in to find the dogs good homes. The GPA alone has helped adopt out more than 65,000 greyhounds since it was established in 1987.

Life Outside the Track

For retired greyhounds, adjusting to civilian life can be a challenge. They've never heard a vacuum cleaner, phone, doorbell, or television. New arrivals often bump into the glass of a sliding door and may be confused by their reflection in a mirror. Stairs are also an obstacle because the dogs live their racing lives entirely on level ground. But with coaxing and affection—and treats—the dogs usually settle into their new environments quickly and easily.

Greyhound owners report that their dogs are among the most lazy and affectionate around. Although the dogs were sprinters in their prime, racing once or twice a week, after they retire, they just want to relax. Most spend their days sprawled out on the sofa, curled up on a bed, or splayed on their backs catching some sun by a window. They're very loving and make terrible watchdogs. Greyhounds rarely bark, and when they do, it sounds more like a whiny "roo, roo" than a menacing "woof!"

Grandiose Greyhounds

Greyhounds have posted some amazing stats over the years. Take a look at some of them:

- A greyhound can lose five pounds in a single race.
- A greyhound in racing condition has only 16 percent body fat, less than half that of dogs of similar size.
- At a gallop, a racing greyhound touches the track surface for only 25 percent of its stride distance.

- A greyhound's heart circulates its entire blood volume five times during a 30-second race.
- Greyhounds come in many colors and variations, including solid, patched, brindled, spotted, ticked, and striped. The least common color is the bluish gray that gives them their name.
- When he traveled, General George Custer usually took 22 greyhounds with him to keep him company and help him hunt.
- Racing greyhounds rarely sit because they've been trained to remain standing while they wait to race. Also, their very muscular hindquarters can make sitting an uncomfortable position for them.

* * *

Dog Show Dos and Don'ts

Do . . . respect the judges' decisions even if you don't agree. The dog show world is small, and the judges will remember you.

Don't . . . bring an aggressive dog into the show ring.

Do . . . hold the lead only in your left hand; if you double-hand the lead, everyone will peg you as an amateur.

Don't . . . make any surgical or cosmetic changes to your dog's appearance; you'll be disqualified.

Leading the Way

On page 26, we explained the early relationship between dogs and the blind. The story continues here, with the tale of how a smart German shepherd and a school in New Jersey have helped blind people become more independent.

The first official guide dog was a female German shepherd named Buddy. She was trained in Switzerland by American expatriate Dorothy Harrison Eustis, who taught German shepherds to be police dogs. Buddy found a home in 1928 when she moved to Tennessee to assist Morris Frank, a blind man living in Nashville. A year before, Frank had read an article that Eustis wrote about dog guides in Germany who assisted blind World War I veterans. He asked Eustis to train a dog for him; in return, Frank agreed to spread the word about Buddy and how she helped him become independent.

The Seeing Eye

While Frank and Buddy traveled the country, showing off the dog's skills, Eustis returned to the United States in 1929 and founded the Seeing Eye, a school to train "Seeing Eye" dogs and to teach blind people to work with the animals. (The name Seeing Eye comes from the Bible: "The seeing eye, the hearing ear; the Lord hath made them both.")

Seeing Eye held its first classes in Morris Frank's hometown of Nashville and graduated 17 canine students within a year. In 1931, the school moved to Morristown, New Jersey.

Becoming a Seeing Eye Dog

Today, the school operates on a 60-acre campus in Morristown, about 35 miles outside of New York City. Seeing Eye breeds most of its own animals—German shepherds, Labrador retrievers, and golden retrievers— although they sometimes take in boxers or other dogs who show exceptional skill or smarts. When the puppies are about 18 months old, they start a training program that lasts four months and teaches them commands and how to walk in a harness. The dogs' handlers even blindfold themselves and walk around town so the animals can begin to learn how to guide the blind.

Human students (both teenagers and adults) spend two to three weeks living at the school where they're matched with a dog, learn the commands, and learn to work as a team with their new canine companions. The Seeing Eye program isn't cheap—students pay $150 up front and $50 per day from then on—

but the cost includes everything from ownership of the dog and training to airfare and expenses while the student is staying at Seeing Eye.

When student and canine are comfortable with each other, they leave the school to take on the world together. Typically, a Seeing Eye dog spends about eight years assisting his human companion. After that time, the dogs' senses start to dull, and they aren't as sharp and alert as they need to be. Masters can keep their dogs as pets or return them to the school, which will find good homes for the dogs to live out their golden years. And it's all thanks to Buddy, whose example forever changed the lives of disabled and visually impaired people everywhere.

* * *

Quote Me

"Dogs never lie about love."

—*Jeffrey Moussaieff Mason*

"No one can fully understand love unless he is owned by a dog."

—*Gene Hill*

"The dog was created especially for children. He is the god of the frolic."

—*Henry Ward Beecher*

Dogfight!

Throughout history, man's best friend has stood by his master's side even when the drums of war start to beat.

The First Great War

Dogs have been part of fighting forces since ancient times, but they first officially joined the military during World War I, when European nations used more than a million dogs on the battlefield. These animals participated on both sides, and they served primarily as guards to prevent soldiers from being surprised by the enemy. They were also used as messengers and rat hunters. (Rats in the trenches were known to carry deadly diseases like typhus and meningitis.)

Dogs assisted the wounded as well. The Red Cross had a corps of Mercy Dogs, who helped track down and carry medicinal supplies to injured soldiers. Other animals were trained to return with something from a wounded person to indicate they'd found him, and German dogs held their leashes in their mouths to indicate when they'd located a fallen soldier. A French dog named Prusco even pulled several men back into the safety of the trenches. Europeans also used Cigarette Dogs; these animals carried bundles of smokes to soldiers on the front lines.

The United States was the only country involved in the conflict that didn't have a war dog program. That would soon change.

World War II

After the attack on Pearl Harbor in 1941, the United States entered World War II, and the next year, the U.S. armed forces created its first dog-training program. The American military worried about sabotage on the home front and thought dogs could help guard bases. Aided by a group of canine-owning patriots, the military started the Dogs for Defense program, which asked citizens to donate their dogs to the war effort. The K-9 Corps took in 19,000 of those dogs, although almost half were eventually winnowed out. In order to make the cut, dogs had to be one to two years old, of neutral markings and color, and weigh 40 to 80 pounds. The breeds that typically passed muster: German shepherds,

 collies, Doberman pinschers, Belgian sheepdogs, and giant schnauzers. Primarily, the dogs guarded military installations, but some, mostly Doberman pinschers, went on combat patrols in the Pacific. There, they kept watch for night-time sneak attacks and acted as scouts. These Dobermans were part of the Marine Corps and were nick-named "Devildogs."

The British also built up a dog program after they discovered that the Germans had deployed some 200,000 dogs to help their war effort. British search-and-rescue dogs dug the wounded out of the rubble of London during the Blitz, and canines acted as messengers, scouts, and guards throughout Europe. Dogs also helped flush out bunkers and find hidden enemy soldiers.

Korea and Beyond

The wars in Korea and Vietnam saw the use of American K-9 units mostly for scouting and guard duty. The dogs were so good at their jobs that the Vietcong paid bounties for military dogs. Today, there are four U.S. sites with memorials dedicated to Vietnam's military dogs: Riverside, California; Fort Benning, Georgia; Port Neches, Texas; and Streamwood, Illinois.

Countries around the world now use military dogs to patrol installations, sniff out bombs or illegal substances, and even help with border patrols. In Iraq and Afghanistan, dogs work at checkpoints and guard military camps. No matter what kind of situations arise, one way or another, it seems there will be dogs by soldiers' sides.

* * *

"No matter how little money and how few possessions you own, having a dog makes you rich."

—*Louis Sabin, writer*

You Know You're a
Dog Lover When . . .

. . . your dog licks your food but you eat it anyway.

. . . you spell out words like "walk" and "treat" even when you're talking to humans.

. . . your dog has a toy box that's so stuffed it won't close.

. . . you and your dog go for car rides just so he can stick his head out the window.

. . . you've left parties or other social gatherings to go home and feed your dog.

. . . your dog has eaten off your dishes more than your guests have.

. . . you buy a king-sized bed so there's room for your dogs.

. . . your dog drinks from the toilet but you let him kiss you anyway.

. . . you buy your dog a Happy Meal at McDonald's. (Hey—he likes the toy!)

. . . you've always got a plastic bag on hand—just in case.

Treat Your Dog Right

On page 40, we told you about the history of dog food. Here's how that story led to the creation of doggy treats and snacks.

No Bones About It

In 1908, the F.H. Bennett Company created bone-shaped biscuits for dogs, the first dog food sold in the United States. The biscuits came in individual packets to preserve their freshness and in various sizes for different breeds. Later called Milk-Bones, the biscuits were made from meat, grains, and cow's milk and were fortified with liver oil, wheat germ, and yeast. Despite their packaging, the high fat content in Milk-Bones often made them turn rancid on store shelves waiting for consumers to buy them. But in 1931, Nabisco bought Bennett's company and used its marketing powers to sell Milk-Bones to more customers.

By the early 1930s, several dog-specific foods had hit the market, so Nabisco advertised Milk-Bones as "a dog's dessert." That way, consumers would buy Milk-Bones in addition to other types of dog food. Thanks to that advertising machine, dog biscuits were no longer a type of food—they were treats.

Healthy Dogs, Healthy Profits

In the years after World War II, many Americans (and their dogs) moved to large cities and suburbs, away from farms and open spaces. Partly as a result of this urban growth, the practice of veterinary medicine became more widespread. Dog owners no longer had the time—or knowledge—to care for every aspect of their pets' health; this task was handed over to licensed veterinarians. And as the well-being of America's furry companions became a more widespread concern for pet owners, several companies were quick to capitalize.

In 1955, Nylabone introduced its first product, a nonedible bone-shaped chew toy designed to satisfy a dog's chewing needs (in place of, say, a pair of designer shoes); the company's product line later expanded to include edible chews and treats. In the early 1960s, Hartz, a leading supplier of bird and fish products, introduced its line of dog supplies, which included snacks like rawhide chews and bones designed to promote good doggy dental health. By the early 1980s, Hartz products could be found in more than 40,000 U.S. stores.

Treats Go Gourmet

Manufacturers continued to expand the range of products. In the late 1970s, William Tyznik, a professor of animal science at Ohio State University, saw some women at a Dairy Queen give a sundae to their dogs. Realizing that ice cream was not good nutrition for dogs (because most dogs are lactose-intolerant), Tyznik whipped up a frozen treat made of soy protein, whey (with the lactose removed), and several vitamins and minerals, and used his own dogs, as his first taste testers. The dogs loved the treat, and Frosty Paws, which was later acquired by Nestlé, can now be found in supermarkets across the country.

At any major pet store today, customers in search of dog biscuits no longer have to choose solely between large Milk-Bones and small Milk-Bones. Options now include organic, vegetarian (contradictory as that may seem), prepared mixes for treats to be baked at home, and treats that look like cookies. (Smaller pet stores and specialized bakeries even offer dog cookies made to order.) Today's top-selling dog treats are Greenies chews, which were introduced in 1998 and are designed to promote dental health and fresh breath. With so many choices on the market, no pooch is ever far from a little something special that will set his tail a-waggin'.

* * *

In the movies and on TV, Lassie was a female dog. But every canine actor who played her was male.

The First
"Last Great Race," Part 2

On page 1, we began the story of the heroic Alaskan Iditarod dogs. Here's how the tail . . . er . . . tale ends.

Guts and Greatness

Wild Bill Shannon handed off the serum in Tolovana at 11 a.m., and over the next five days, 19 other sled dog teams carried the serum. The last two were the most famous.

Leonhard Seppala and his team, led by Togo, were already well known for setting records in dog sled races. Seppala was the most skilled musher of his day, and Togo was (and still is) considered by many to be the greatest dog to ever run the Iditarod trail. Small for a husky, Togo was fast and hardy, but he was also courageous in the face of danger and smart enough to make good decisions during a race.

Seppala was already in Nome when he was asked to pick up the serum. He and his dogs traveled 150 miles east and met musher Henry Ivanoff, who handed it off. Seppala turned around and immediately headed back to Nome. By the time his team stopped at the next relay point, they'd covered more than 250 miles. (Most members of the relay traveled about 30 miles.) Togo had a sprained foot, and they'd pushed through terrible storms. Yet the dogs never gave up. On the way back to Nome, the team had been caught in strong winds that delayed them. Seppala had to decide whether to risk a shortcut across the ice floes in Norton Sound or go around them and lose precious time. A wrong decision meant he and the dog team could lose not only the serum but their lives. Trusting Togo, the musher took the shortcut, and the husky confidently led his team over the sound, choosing only patches of solid ice, until they reached the safety of land.

Guts and Glory

At the second-to-last relay point, the small town of Bluff, Seppala's assistant, Gunnar Kaasen, took over. His lead dog was a young Siberian husky named Balto. There were about 50 miles of cold wilderness between the serum and the patients who needed it. So Kaasen and his team took off for Nome. Along the way, blizzards whipped up wild winds and snow. Kaasen's sled turned over, and he lost the package of serum. Panicked, Kaasen took off his mittens and searched for the package on his hands and knees in the snow. He finally found it, retied it to the sled, and Balto and the rest of the dogs raced on.

Different stories explain what happened next. Some say that because all of the dog teams had made such good time, they weren't expected so early at the final relay point in Point Safety, about 22 miles from Nome, and the final musher was asleep when Balto and his team arrived. Kaasen felt that it would take too long for the musher to wake up and harness his dogs, so he decided to continue on. Other accounts say that Kaasen skipped the relay altogether because he wanted the glory of arriving in Nome with the serum. No matter the details, Balto led his team to Nome. On February 2, at about 5:30 a.m., Kaasen knocked on Dr. Welch's door and offered up the 300,000 units of serum. Waiting on the street were the exhausted dogs who'd covered 53 miles in just seven and a half hours.

All's Well That Ends Well

In total, the 20 volunteer dog sled teams had traveled 674 dangerous miles in about five and a half days. The serum arrived in time to stop the epidemic.

News of the dog teams' valor spread around the world, and when telegraph operators reported that Kaasen and Balto had delivered the serum to Dr. Welch, the pair became heroes. A film crew in Nome asked Kaasen to re-enact his arrival while the citizens of Nome cheered him on. Balto went on to star in a Hollywood film, and Kaasen took his dog team on the vaudeville circuit. Heroes can be quickly forgotten, though, and in the late 1920s, Balto and several other members of his dog team ended up hungry and mistreated at a zoo in Los Angeles. That's when George Kimble, a businessman from Cleveland, stepped in and rescued them. He established the Balto Fund and appealed to Cleveland's youngest dog lovers. The city's schoolchildren raised $2,000 to bring the dogs to Ohio, where they lived out their days—happy and well-fed—at Cleveland's Metroparks Zoo.

Seppala's dog Togo found fame, too, though Seppala always felt that Balto's accomplishments overshadowed his. In 1926, Seppala's team was invited to New York's Madison Square Garden to race around the ice arena, and explorer Roald Amundsen awarded Togo a gold medal. Togo's body is now on display at the Iditarod race head-quarters in Wasilla, Alaska; Balto's remains can be seen at the Cleveland Museum of Natural History. And every year, dog sled teams race in honor of all the heroes who beat time to save the people of Nome.

* * *

The Rottweiler breed is thought to have descended from the dogs that guarded camps and herds belonging to ancient Roman legions.

Man Ray's Best Friend

William Wegman never intended to become known for his dog photographs. He wanted to be a conceptual artist, but then a Weimaraner moved into his home, invaded his art, and made Wegman more famous than his "serious" work ever could.

Born in Massachusetts in 1943, William Wegman grew up in the small town of East Longmeadow, the son of a factory worker. He loved painting and art and went to college at the University of Illinois, earning a master of fine arts degree. He then began teaching art at the college level. Wegman gave up painting early on, believing there was no longer a market for it, and in 1970 took up conceptual art, a style in which the work's concept takes precedence over its beauty. The story goes that he was inspired by the similarities between peppercorns in a piece of salami and the gemstones in one of his rings. He set up a scene with the food, ring, and some circles he'd drawn; took a photo; and a conceptual artist was born.

Starring . . . Man Ray

It wasn't conceptual art that would make him famous, however. In 1971, Wegman moved to Los Angeles—then the center of the conceptual art world—and met a silver-gray Weimaraner, whom he bought for $35 and named Man Ray (in honor of the famous 20th-century painter and photographer). Wegman continued working on conceptual pieces; he also began making art videos. But Man Ray always seemed to wander into the shots. At first, Wegman tried to shoo the dog away, but he soon realized that Man Ray had real star quality and could make the shots more interesting.

Wegman started taking snapshots and videos of Man Ray, first in realistic poses—sitting on pedestals or licking milk off of the floor—and then in more surreal scenarios: dressed up like Cinderella, sporting an elephant's trunk, or watching television. The dog was photogenic, and his deadpan demeanor worked well for Wegman's photos. By the end of the 1970s, Wegman and Man Ray were famous. The artist participated in two one-man shows, and Man Ray's videos occasionally showed up as sketches on *Saturday Night Live*.

Man of the Year

With fame came some frustration. Wegman wanted to be recognized as a serious artist, not "that dog guy." In the late 1970s, he took a break from photographing his most famous subject. He concentrated on his own drawings and says he became "a strange, sad, lonely, hibernating sort of person." But in 1978, Man Ray was stricken with prostate cancer and went into a coma. Wegman was devastated when the vet suggested putting Man Ray down, and the artist refused. Instead, he treated the Weimaraner with antibiotics. Eventually, the dog recovered.

After nearly losing his muse, Wegman fully embraced

his role as dog artist. For the next four years, he took numerous photos of the dog, and the pair became even more famous. In 1982, the year Man Ray died, *Time* magazine named the dog "Man of the Year."

Another Fa(y)mous Pooch

In the first years after Man Ray's death, Wegman concentrated on more traditional art. He drew and painted, and didn't include dogs in his work at all. But in 1985, he fell for another Weimaraner, a little brown puppy he named Fay Ray (an homage to Man Ray and to Fay Wray, the actress of *King Kong* fame). Soon, he started to photograph her.

Fay became almost as famous as her predecessor. She appeared in numerous photos and videos and even guest-starred on *Sesame Street*. Today, Wegman lives in Massachusetts and teaches photography at Boston's Massachusetts College of Art.

* * *

Myth-conception

Myth: Saint Bernards wear kegs of brandy around their necks when they go out to rescue stranded travelers.
Fact: They never have. The popular idea comes from a series of paintings by Sir Edwin Landseer in the 1800s that depicted the dogs wearing brandy casks.

Speak!

*Howls, growls, and barks . . . what's your dog
trying to say? Here's what the experts think.*

Woof

Most vets and animal behaviorists believe that dogs have
distinct barks to communicate different things. Of course,
a dog's personality will always affect his tone and volume,
but here are some of the most common meanings:

- A series of low-frequency barks often means a dog is
  feeling defensive of his territory, his master, or himself.
- High-pitched, repetitive barks are the sound of a dis-
  tressed dog.
- Gentle woofs mean your dog is feeling content or is
  anticipating something enjoyable . . . like a meal.
- A rumbling bark (often preceded by a deep growl)
  means your pup perceives a threat.

Grrrrr

Generally speaking, a dog will not bite when a simple growl
will do. More complicated than the other sounds, growls are
one of the subtlest ways that canines communicate.
Sometimes dogs growl while playing. Other times, they
growl in pain. Typically, though, they growl in five ways:

- A soft, low-pitched growl is a warning.
- A low-pitched growl that leads to a bark means a dog is upset and ready to defend himself.
- A mid- to high-pitched growl combined with barking means a dog is intimidated and frightened, but will fight back if pushed.
- An undulating growl that goes from midrange to high midrange—sometimes combined with quick bursts of barking—means a dog is scared and feeling unsure. If further antagonized, the dog may run . . . or he may fight back.
- A noisy growl that shows no teeth usually means your pooch is playing. Occasionally, a series of stuttering barks accompanies this gleeful growl.

Awroooo

Howling is most often associated with wolves, but domestic dogs do it too. In the wild, it's typically used to reconnect with a pack, so domestic dogs howl to connect with their owners or another animal. Usually, though, howling in a domestic dog requires a trigger, such as a siren or another howler.

* * *

Mark your calendar: June 22 is "take your dog to work day." (We suggest you get your boss's OK first, though.)

My Dog Has Fleece

You're knitting with what?

Reasons to Bark

Dedicated dog hair knitters know that other people think they're weird. Says one knitter, "When you first tell your friends that the garment you're wearing was previously worn by your dog, you're bound to get some raised eyebrows." Some even ask, with eyes wide, "How many dogs have to be killed to make a sweater?" But for the knitters, it's all in a day's work. They've even come up with a new name for their materials. By combining *chien*, the French word for "dog," with the name of another natural hair fiber, angora, they've coined a new name for dog-hair creations—*Chiengora*. In fact, one knitter insists that dog hair should be considered a luxury fiber, like all the others that come from humble origins, including cashmere (goat), angora (rabbit), and mohair (also goat).

The hardcore dog lovers who practice this art make sweaters, hats, mittens, and even pantsuits from the hair of their beloved pets. They report that chiengora is "soft and fluffy, incredibly warm, and it sheds water." Besides that, dog lovers have sentimental reasons for knitting with chiengora: they'll always have a memento of their favorite canine pal.

Shaggy Dog Yarn

The key to knitting with dog hair is length. Pet owners shouldn't cut fur from their pets, mainly because those fibers would be too short. You can still knit with these short hairs, but they have to be mixed with wool or other fibers to hold together.

The best dog hair is the long fiber your pooch sheds on his own. It should be about two inches long. Plus, the longer the dog hair, the better the results. So collies, poodles, golden retrievers, and others like them make the best hair.

The Hair Harvest

The best way to collect the hair is to remove it from brushes and combs. Even with the hairiest dog, it can take several years to collect enough hair for a major project like a sweater or a blanket. Experts disagree about how you should store the hair as you gather it. Some say that a dry paper bag is best, but others suggest a tightly sealed plastic bag to keep out fleas and moths. "Moths love dog hair," says one knitter who recommends ziplock bags. Regardless, paper grocery bags make a good standard of measure:

a knitted sweater takes about two bags of hair, a vest about one, and a hat about a third of a bag.

Once you have your big bags of hair, how do you turn it into yarn? Dog hair requires gentle hand-spindling with a weighted drop spindle—none of those newfangled machines like the spinning wheel. The result comes from twisting the hairs around each other. And the good thing about fibers like dog hair is that if the yarn breaks, you just fluff up the end and begin again, adding fibers.

Odds and . . . Odds

- If you have a multicolored dog, experts suggest keeping the colors somewhat separate to give an interesting graduated color effect.
- Mixing the hair together yields a uniform gray-beige color.
- Like the dogs they came from, dog-hair garments should be hand-washed—not thrown into a washing machine. Unlike the dogs, the fabrics can be dry-cleaned. Dog-hair garments can last as long as 20 years.

* * *

Out of Dog's Way

During World War I, soldiers who impeded messenger dogs as they ran to and from their assigned posts could face court-martial.

The AKC
By the Numbers

For more than 120 years, the American Kennel Club (AKC) has been the official record keeper and "advocate for the purebred dog." Here are some vital stats.

2

Number of "most prestigious" dog shows sponsored by the AKC: the Westminster Kennel Club Show, held in New York City every February, and the AKC/Eukanuba National Championship, an invitation-only event for the top dogs on the world's dog show circuit. The AKC also sanctions more than 18,000 smaller contests annually.

12

Number of dog clubs that united in 1884 to form the Club of Clubs—which became the American Kennel Club. The AKC's main purpose then was to create a registry of purebred dogs, known as the Stud Book. Over the years, the Stud Book has included information on millions of dogs. Today, there are 584 organizations that meet the requirements of AKC membership (which includes holding sanctioned events that award AKC titles and having delegates who represent the club at quarterly meetings). There are approximately 5,000 additional local groups that hold events under the umbrella of the AKC—from national and local clubs dedicated to one specific breed to those devoted to particular skills (such as agility, obedience, tracking, field trials, lure coursing, and herding tests and trials).

$25 (plus $2 for each puppy)

Cost to register a newborn litter of purebred puppies with the AKC. Although the title "AKC registered" is widely thought to signify purity and quality, it really only assures that someone has bred two dogs of the same breed, filled out the proper form, and paid the fee. The registry tracks that a purebred parental chain has not been broken, but it requires no information on the health of the parents or pups or on the expertise of the breeder.

85

The percentage of genes common to dogs and humans. Because of this close genetic relationship, canines and humans are also subject to many of the same diseases.

118

Years the monthly *AKC Gazette* magazine—the official magazine of the AKC—has been published. (It first hit the presses in January 1889.) The AKC's *Complete Dog Book*—considered the bible of dog guides, with descriptions and the official standards for every recognized breed—was first published in 1929 and is currently in its 20th edition.

157

Breeds officially recognized by the AKC. Although other registries list approximately 400 breeds, the AKC recognizes only those that meet specific requirements, including having an active national breed club that maintains its own registry and a "substantial, sustained nationwide interest and activity in the breed." The 157 breeds are further subdivided into seven groups based on the purpose for which each breed was developed: sporting, hound (with two categories—sight hounds and scent hounds), working, terrier, toy, non-sporting (often called companion dogs), and herding.

5,000

Inspections of boarding kennels that the AKC's Compliance Division performs every year. That's more than the ASPCA and USDA combined.

123,760

Labrador retriever pups registered in 2006. Labradors have been the most popular dog in the United States for more than 15 years, with almost three times the number of new registrations for the second-most popular breed, the Yorkshire terrier (with 48,346). German shepherds are third (with 43,575), and the golden retriever is fourth (with 42,962). Those four breeds alone comprised about 30 percent of the nearly 900,000 dogs registered in 2006.

3,100,000
Dogs enrolled in the AKC Companion Animal Recovery program, a microchip-implanting system dedicated to reuniting lost pets with their owners. More than 300,000 lost dogs have been found with the help of microchip tracking. A lifetime enrollment of the microchip number in the AKC database costs only $12.50.

* * *

A Dog Tag's Life
During the Civil War, only 58 percent of the soldiers killed in action were positively identified, and many servicemen worried that their families would never know their fates. So soldiers started writing their names on pieces of paper or on handkerchiefs and pinning them to their clothes before they went into battle. Some even carved small wooden disks with their names on them, drilled a hole in the disk, and hung it from their necks with a piece of string. Others made ID tags by grinding off one side of a coin and etching their name on it. Eventually, retail merchants started selling metal disks called "soldier pins" that were made of silver or gold and had the soldier's name and unit etched into them. Because dogs wore similar identification tags, soldiers started calling their ID tags "dog tags."

Thank You Barry Much

*In the 350 years since they were first bred, Saint Bernards
have rescued more than 2,000 people in the Swiss Alps.
The most famous lifesaver was a dog named Barry.*

Taking the High Road

High in the Swiss Alps, 8,000 feet above sea level, is the
Hospice of the Great Saint Bernard. The monestary was
built during the Middle Ages by Saint Bernard himself as a
stopover for travelers along the mountain pass between
Italy and northern Europe. For hundreds of years, the
Great Saint Bernard Pass was one of the few routes over
the Alps, and it was widely used until a tunnel was built in
the 20th century.

The early trail was so dangerous and narrow that
groups going in opposite directions—in wagons or on
foot—couldn't pass each other safely. Ice, deep snow,
bitter cold, blizzards, and avalanches were constant
threats, and to make matters worse, gangs of robbers
roamed the pass, menacing and murdering unwary and
unprepared travelers. The monks who lived at the hospice dedicated their lives to helping people in trouble by
searching out the lost and injured and providing them
with hot meals and a warm place to stay.

145

Good Breeding

In the 17th century, the monks started breeding the first Saint Bernard dogs, both to protect themselves and to help with rescues. The dogs turned out to be rescuers without equal. They could smell a human two miles away, even against a howling wind, and detect a victim buried under more than 10 feet of snow. They could even sense an impending blizzard 20 minutes before it started and knew when an avalanche was about to occur. These unusual skills combined with their gentle dispositions, great strength, and stamina made the dogs the perfect companions for rescue work in the pass.

Barry to the Rescue

The greatest of them all, though, was Barry. Born at the monastery in 1800, Barry was a light, small-boned dog who developed some incredible rescue skills. When he sensed a storm coming, he insisted on being allowed outside and immediately started searching for snow-bound travelers. He could dig a man out of the snow and lead him back to the warmth of the hospice under most circumstances, but when his best efforts failed, he had the intelligence to run back to the monastery and get help. If accompanied by a rescue party, Barry would lie down next to the lost or injured person, providing warmth until help arrived. Over the years, he saved more than 40 lives.

On one life-saving mission, Barry and the monks found a young boy trapped and unconscious on a steep, icy ledge. Heavy snow made it impossible for the monks to climb to his rescue, but Barry crawled upward until he reached the child, lying down beside him and licking his face until he regained consciousness. The boy wrapped his arms around his rescuer's neck, and Barry dragged him safely down the ledge to the waiting monks.

The Stuff of Legend

As tales of Barry's rescues spread throughout Europe, he morphed into a legendary hero, and many of his rescues were embellished. One of these stories told of Barry finding a mother and infant in the snow. The mother was dying, but she wrapped her baby in her shawl and tied the shawl around Barry's neck. She died, but her baby was saved. Another myth says that Barry died while trying to rescue a soldier who, thinking the dog was a wolf, killed him with his sword. In reality, Barry retired in 1812 and lived out the rest of his life on a farm until he died in 1814.

Forever Barry

Today, Barry's body is preserved and on permanent display at the Museum of Natural History in Berne, Switzerland. Roads have replaced the Great Saint Bernard Pass, and helicopters now do Barry's work, finding skiers and mountain climbers in need of rescue.

The remaining Saint Bernards spend summers with the few monks left at the hospice; they're a tourist attraction now and still a beloved part of Swiss culture. The rest of the world may call the dogs Saint Bernards, but the Swiss call them *Barryhunds* or "Barry dogs." And to this day, the strongest and most beautiful puppy born in every litter at the hospice is christened "Barry."

* * *

The Name Game

Dachshunds: In German, the name means "badger dog," and dachshunds, with their short legs and long bodies, were originally bred to flush badgers and other underground animals from their holes.

Bloodhounds: Back in the Middle Ages, these dogs belonged exclusively to nobles and other high-ranking folks. For that reason, they were originally called "blooded" (or, aristocratic) hounds.

Luxury Lodging

For the rich and famous, traditional
kennel boarding simply will not do.

Urban Luxury

If you want to spoil your dog, the Ritzy Canine Carriage House, located in a 19th-century brownstone on East 40th Street in New York City, is the place to do it. The facility's posh rooms, delectable meals, and hands-on service have made it one of New York's most lavish pet resorts. Doggy boarders can stay anywhere from one night to 2½ months, and while they're there, the animals want for nothing. Ritzy Canine offers massages, pawdicures, a fitness center, room service, and even a plush Presidential Suite where your pooch can relax in his own private room and watch TV. The dogs have plenty of exercise during their stays, but they don't have to go onto New York's mean streets to get it. Ritzy Canine has its own outdoor garden on the building's roof—and the garden is sectioned off into shaded and unshaded areas, to suit your dog's mood. All this luxury doesn't come cheap: rates range from $60 per night for a small dog (under 20 pounds) in a shared room to $175 per night for the Presidential Suite. (Pawdicures, massages, and room service are extra.)

A Southern Spa

For the health- and calorie-conscious, Club Pet (which proudly calls itself the only five-star hotel in West Virginia) offers overnight guests a fitness program—from low impact exercise to strenuous Olympic workouts. Their chef will spoil these prized guests with his gourmet menu and can tailor meals to suit special diets. Pets have the freedom to roam in and out of their luxury rooms, and each decorated suite, complete with a cozy bed, is warmed in the winter and cooled in the summer. Soothing music plays throughout Club Pet to keep pets relaxed. If your dog prefers movies to music, he can go back to his suite where a TV and DVD player await. When he's ready to jump back into canine civilization, Fido can join the other guests at Critter Park, a fenced-in grassy area where dogs are encouraged to play. Add massages, soothing baths, and pedicures, and your pet will look and feel great!

Rustic Lodging

At its two locations in Albuquerque, Canine Country Club provides palatial accommodations that even the most finicky Fido will enjoy—and lots of love and head scratching to make him feel at home. Standard accommodations cost $21 per night and consist of spacious two-sided rooms with floors that are heated during the winter. Pets sleep on lamb's-wool blankets, and if you want to splurge ($34 to $43 per night), Canine Country Club offers special suites (called casitas) that include a living room, patio, child-size bed, and TV/DVD. Couch potato pooches can indulge in as much television and music as they like, while the fitness-minded can use treadmills to keep in shape during their stay. For an extra dollar per indulgence, your pet can go to "Yappy Hour" where he can enjoy "doggy ice cream" (nondairy yogurt), a peanut-butter-filled Kong toy, or an all-beef hot dog.

Friendly Farmstay

Lucie's Farm in Worcester, England, is an exclusive dog resort. The hosts allow only a few guests at a time, which means lots of personal attention. The facility's 57 acres of land allow for plenty of room for running and romping around. And because Lucie's Farm is an actual, running farm, their chef uses only the best ingredients like farm-reared beef, freshly picked vegetables, and freshly laid eggs in the guests' cuisine.

The accommodations include comfortable rooms with temperature-controlled floors so pets can choose a warm or cool spot to suit their fancies. Lucie's Farm also offers "healing touch" massages in their Zen Den, hydrotherapy in the pool, and acupuncture performed by a veterinarian. And while you're away, you won't have to wonder how your dog is doing: Lucie's Farm will e-mail you daily with a digital photo and a diary of your pet's visit.

Foods Only a Dog Could Love

Check out the top five ingredients in some of your pooch's favorite snacks. Yum!

Pig's Ears
Well, dried pig's ears—unless your pooch prefers cow's ears, which are made from . . . cow's ears. Really, that's it.

Dentabones
Wheat gluten, heat-treated wheat flour, toasted whole rice, gelatin, and glycerin

T Bonz
Ground wheat, corn gluten meal, water, wheat flour, and ground yellow corn

Beggin' Strips
Ground wheat, corn gluten meal, wheat flour, ground yellow corn, and water (or sugar, depending on the flavor)

Snausages
Wheat flour, beef, soy flour, corn syrup, and water sufficient for processing

Greenies Smart Biscuit

Wheat flour, wheat gluten, rice flour, oat flour, and chicken fat

Liv-A-Snaps

Wheat flour, animal liver, soy flour, oat hulls, and tri-calcium phosphate

* * *

The High Life

When the canine superstars of the Westminster Dog Show arrive in the Big Apple, the city goes all out. At night, the tower of the Empire State Building is bathed in purple and gold (the official colors of the Westminster Kennel Club), and even the M&Ms at Madison Square Garden, where the show is held, are appropriately colored. Shop windows sport dog themes, and more than a dozen hotels open their fancy doors to the contestants and their entourages. The Hotel Pennsylvania has hosted many a Westminster winner and prides itself on its pet-friendly amenities, including a welcome package of dog treats and supplies, a dog spa and comfort station, a veterinarian on the premises, and a dedicated doggy concierge to handle all the mundane details that go along with their trip. Bars in the area offer "Yappy Hour" specials such as the "Black Russian Wolfhound," "Naughty Dog," "Furry Navel," and "Hair of the Dog."

Pooches Extraordinaire

*Some dogs fetch; others sit. But these seemingly
ordinary canines do some extraordinary tricks!*

Surf's Up!

As the early morning swells roll onto Southern
California's Ventura Beach, surfers take to the water, pad-
dling out to wait for the best wave. There's one surfer in
the lineup, though, who needs a little help. Nine-year-old
Buddy, a mostly white Jack Russell terrier who's been surfing since he was two, can't paddle out alone, so his owner
(and surfing pal) Bruce Hooker helps him along. But once
Buddy sets up for a wave, he takes off on his own. Hooker
says that he never intentionally tried to teach Buddy to
surf; the dog just loved to be with him and, one day,
hopped on a board and was infected with "surf stoke."

Buddy can ride a short board, long board, and body
board, and he also likes to ride tandem with Hooker. He's
got great form, always crouching low to maintain his bal-
ance and control, and he's a big believer in safety first:
Buddy always wears a life jacket when he hits the beach.

The Artiste

Another Jack Russell terrier, this one from New York, has

made a name for herself in the art world. Eight-year-old Tillie—her full name is Tillamook Cheddar, after the Oregon brand of cheese that her owner loved to eat as a child—started painting when she was just six months old, when her owner, F. Bowman Hastie III, noticed Tillie scratching on a pad of paper. He covered the pad with carbon paper, and Tillie continued to scratch until she'd completed her artwork. Three months later, she had her first art show.

Today, she mostly works in paint-coated transfer paper to create her abstract artwork. Hastie covers a canvas with the paper, and Tillie scratches until Hastie decides she's done. When Hastie peels away the transfer paper, the canvas reflects the dog's efforts. So far, Tillie's work has been shown in 16 solo exhibitions and 20 group exhibitions. Her paintings hang in galleries around the world, and she's made about $100,000. She's even collaborated with human artists, been the subject of a coffee-table book, and appeared on various radio and television talk shows.

Born to Skate(board)

Tyson—a brown-and-white bulldog from Huntington Beach, California—is a self-taught skateboarding champ. He started boarding in 2001 when he was just a year old, first

in his owners' backyard and then on the sidewalks out front. Soon, he was cruising around the neighborhood on four wheels. His owners say they don't know what made Tyson choose the skateboard or how he learned to do it, but he's so good at it and has so much fun that they believe he was "born to skate." His skating sessions can last from a few minutes to a few hours, and he's been known to ride for more than a mile. Tyson's talent has earned him an agent, a sponsor (Bulldog Skateboards), and parts in several movie and TV productions, including *The Lords of Dogtown*, *American Idol*, and *MTV TRL*. He's also got his own Web site and MySpace page.

* * *

Hot Dog!

In 2005, Los Angeles entrepreneur Ralph Diaz asked himself this question: Why didn't the city have a nightspot that welcomed singles and their canine friends? So he opened SkyBark, a roof-top nightclub where humans and dogs could kick back, have a drink, and socialize. There's even a bone-shaped dog pool, a full-service bar (which offers both standard drinks and specially made vitamin water cocktails for the dogs), and a deejay.

It's not all fun and games, though. Every event at the club includes a silent auction that benefits a local animal rescue selected by Diaz and his staff.

Paws on the Page

Can you name the literary dogs described below?

1. In Laura Ingalls Wilder's *Little House on the Prairie*, published in 1935, this dog is nearly lost when the Ingalls family crosses a swollen creek.

2. These dogs—a Labrador and an English bull terrier—go on an "incredible journey" through the Canadian wilderness (accompanied by a Siamese cat named Tao) in search of their lost human family.

3. This oft-slobbering boarhound is one of several pets belonging to the lovable giant Hagrid in J. K. Rowling's Harry Potter series.

4. Aggressive and angry, Bill Sikes in *Oliver Twist* doesn't take very good care of this dog, his pet bull terrier.

5. Dorothy Gale and this little terrier go on an amazing adventure in L. Frank Baum's 1900 classic.

6. *Bridge to Terabithia*, first published in 1977, tells the story of Jesse Aarons and Leslie Burke, two lonely kids who create a magical imaginary land in the forest. One of their kingdom's royals is this dog.

7. The Darlings of J. M. Barrie's 1904 play (officially published in 1911) *Peter Pan* employ this Newfoundland to watch over their children.

8. Jack London's *Call of the Wild* tells the story of this Saint Bernard/collie mix. In the 1920s and 1930s, several European countries, including Italy and Yugoslavia banned the book, calling it "radical" and too socialist.

9. The tragic *A Dog of Flanders* was first published in 1872 and told the tale of this dog and Nello, his poverty-stricken young master who lives outside Antwerp. Although set in Belgium, the book is incredibly popular in Japan, where it has been turned into a cartoon.

10. This canine narrates Rudyard Kipling's *Thy Servant a Dog*, published in 1930.

See the answers on page 226.

Puppy Padres

The New Skete monks, who live near Cambridge, New York,
train some of the best-behaved dogs in Christendom.

O Brothers, Where Art Thou?

The order of New Skete began in 1966 when a small
group of monks broke away from the mainstream
Franciscans to pursue a more orthodox lifestyle. (*Skete*
means "monastery" in Greek, but the brothers actually
named themselves after a monastery in Egypt that was
located in the Skete desert.) After a six-month planning
session in northern Pennsylvania, the brothers found a
perfect site for their new monastery: a broken-down farm
in Cambridge, New York. They converted it into a running, self-sustaining monastery, but soon found that they
were too conspicuous in the town—there were even
rumors that they were a group of men dodging the
Vietnam draft. So they moved to 500 hilly, rocky acres
outside of town.

The terrain wasn't appropriate for farming, so the
monks tried many other jobs, from mail-order meat sales
to book publishing. Finally they found a calling in breeding and training German shepherd puppies. On their Web
site, the monks state, "In our work, we have tried to utilize

the creative talents of our members in a way that not only supports us financially, but which witnesses to the spiritual values that we live by."

New Skete Dogma

To train the dogs, the monks use discipline and repetition, a regimen that's part of their own life and studies. They also heap praise on their charges and believe that there are no bad dogs—only animals who haven't been trained properly. Their methods are sometimes controversial (some people don't like how aggressive the padres are with their animals), but they can be salvation for the worst-behaved dogs. Take Rory, for example. This six-month-old German shepherd puppy was brought to New Skete by her owner because she was so hard to handle: she fought with the leash, jumped on everything and everyone around her, and wouldn't obey simple commands. After the monks' rigorous training program—which includes direct eye contact, forced submissions, and vocal commands—Rory was so well behaved that her owner hardly recognized her.

Rory is just one of the successes the monks have had, and dog owners aren't the only ones who've noticed. In 2007, the International Association of Canine Professionals (a group for people who work with dogs) recognized the monks' contributions and honored them with an award for "a lifetime of dedication to dogs and their training." The padres have also appeared on an Animal Planet TV special and have published three books about dog training.

Get 'Em While They're Hot

All this recognition makes the dogs the monks breed very popular, which also makes the procedures for selection strict. Prospective owners must fill out a detailed application form that includes questions about why they want a puppy, what dogs they've owned previously, and even what dog training books they've read. This form allows the monks to place puppies with owners who match the dogs' personalities—a policy the friars believe accounts for the many successful matches they've created. The screening process also includes interviews with the monks. Despite these criteria, the monks of New Skete always have more applicants than they do pups.

For people who can't get a New Skete puppy (and who live near Cambridge or can travel there), the monks will train other dogs too. They offer a four-week, $1,300 course that includes room, board, and schooling for the pup, as well as a seminar for the owner so that he or she can continue with the lessons after the pair goes home.

After more than three decades of dog training, the monks at New Skete are a godsend to dog owners around the country. They also enjoy the work. Said one of the brothers, "Working with dogs is . . . something that I call a blessing and an enrichment to my own vocation."

* * *

Eating lots of snow can give a dog hypothermia. On winter hikes, bring along lukewarm water for your pet to drink.

Sunday Morning Mutts

*Ever since Buster Brown showed up in the comics with a bulldog,
Sunday morning strips just haven't been complete without dogs.*

Tige

- *Buster Brown*, one of the earliest newspaper comic
  strips, debuted in 1902 and told of the adventures of a
  mischievous little boy. Buster's dog Tige was the first
  talking pet in American comics.
- In 1904, Buster and Tige became mascots for the Brown
  Shoe Company, a Missouri-based business that made
  Buster Brown children's shoes. The boy and his dog also
  appeared in one of the company's jingles: "That's my
  dog Tige! He lives in a shoe. I'm Buster Brown. Look
  for me in there, too!"

Snoopy

- Charles Schulz wanted to name Snoopy "Sniffy" but
  changed his mind after he discovered that a character
  in another comic strip had that name.
- When *Peanuts* debuted in 1950, Snoopy was Charlie
  Brown's silent dog companion, but two years later,
  Schulz started verbalizing the dog's musings in balloons,
  giving Snoopy a personality more like a human's.

Snoopy then went on to do some very human-like things. He's been a writer, an Olympic figure skater, an attorney, an astronaut, and a World War I flying ace.

- Snoopy is the official NASA mascot of aerospace safety and the mascot of the U.S. Air Force Technical Control—he appears on the agency's official emblem. U.S. astronauts call their helmets "Snoopy caps" because the helmets have a white center and black sides, like Snoopy's head.

Marmaduke

- Marmaduke is one of the few dogs to have his own strip. It debuted in 1954 and currently runs in more than 600 newspapers around the world.
- *Marmaduke* is translated into several languages: in Italian, the dog is called Sansone; in German, he's Archibald; and in Swedish, he's Leopold.
- Marmaduke is the spokesdog for several charities, including the American Cancer Society's annual "Paws for a Cause" dog walk-a-thon.

Odie

- Odie first showed up in *Garfield* on August 8, 1978, two months after the birth of the strip. Originally, he belonged to character Jon Arbuckle's roommate, but when the roommate disappeared from the comic, Odie became Jon's de facto pet.

- Unlike all the other animals in the strip, Odie never has thought balloons, and he doesn't speak. He's smart, though, and may have a secret life: one strip showed him listening to classical music and reading *War and Peace* as soon as Garfield and Jon left the house.

Dogbert
- Creator Scott Adams wanted to name Dogbert, Dilbert's evil-minded pet, Dildog, but editors talked him into changing the name.
- According to the official *Dilbert* site, Dogbert's ambition is to "conquer the world and enslave all humans."

Earl
- Debuting in 1994, *Mutts* follows the adventures and philosophical musings of Earl the dog and his companion Mooch the cat.
- On the advice of Charles Schulz, *Mutts* creator Patrick McDonnell named Earl after his own Jack Russell terrier.
- *Mutts* often uses its title panel—the big panel on Sunday comics—to spoof covers of classic comics like *Dick Tracy* and *Popeye*.

Poncho
- Poncho, the main character of *Pooch Café*, gathers with his fellow mutts at a top-secret location to discuss the important issues of dog-dom—like kibble and squirrels. But *Pooch Café*'s creator, Paul Gilligan, doesn't own a dog.

K-9 to 5

Busy dog parents often fret over leaving their favorite canines home alone all day. But now there is an alternative that allows those energetic pups to get out of the doghouse. Here are the ABCs of it.

Aggressive dogs aren't suited for the doggy day care regime.

Bus service is sometimes available to pick up pooches.

Call your local Humane Society for a doggy day care referral.

Dogs must be interviewed by the facility management to make sure they fit in.

Every dog over six months old has to be spayed or neutered.

Feeding is part of the daily routine.

Grooming is also available at most doggy day care facilities.

Hiking and swimming are just two of the activities offered by some doggy day care centers.

I.D. tags and dog licenses are required.

Just don't settle for any old doggy day care; personally visit the sites and ask questions.

Know if your chosen facility is clean and organized.

Local pet store managers may be a good source for doggy day care recommendations.

Make sure the facility's environment is stimulating, healthy, and safe.

Nap time or quiet time in the afternoon ensures that your pup will not burn out from too much activity.

Older dogs may not be good candidates for doggy day care because the environment is usually louder and more playful than they're used to.

Proof of current shots and vaccinations—rabies, distemper, and bordatella—are necessary.

Qualified doggy day care employees will be knowledgeable in dog behavior and experienced in handling animals.

Rates run, on average, about $25 per day.

Spa services, including doggy massages, are sometimes available for pooches who need pampering.

Talk to other pet parents when searching for a qualified doggy day care.

Use your local phone book or try an online search when you first begin to look.

Veterinarians must provide a written statement that your pet is healthy and that his shots are up to date.

Web cams are available at some facilities so pet parents can see exactly what their canine pals are up to.

'Xercise and socialization are features of any good doggy day care.

Younger dogs usually adjust well to the energetic day care environment.

Zzzzzzzz . . . at the end of the day, pups should be good and tired—just like their pet parents.

Don't Feed It to Fido!

*Dogs will eat anything—but here are 10 things
your pooch should never consume.*

1. Chocolate

The rumors are true: chocolate can be deadly to dogs. A
chemical called theobromine, which makes chocolate
bitter, is toxic to them. It can cause diarrhea, muscle
tremors, vomiting, and seizures. The darker the chocolate,
the more dangerous it is for your pooch.

2. Garlic and onions

These both contain chemicals that can damage your dog's
red blood cells when ingested in large doses (the small
amounts in some dog foods are okay). Dogs who've been
poisoned by onions or garlic can have trouble breathing,
will be lethargic, and can become anemic.

3. Macadamia nuts

They're delicious for you, but poisonous to your pooch.
Dogs who eat macadamia nuts sometimes experience
stomach pain, vomiting, and weakness in their legs. No
one seems to know what chemical causes this reaction, but
some dogs can get sick after eating as few as six nuts. The

dogs will recover, usually with no lasting effects, after the macadamia nuts leave their system, but it's best not to take the chance.

4. Alcohol

Alcohol, even beer, can have a negative effect on dogs. There's debate over whether or not alcohol will actually kill a canine, but it's certain that dogs get drunk much more quickly than humans. So keep the booze out of reach.

5. Caffeine

Caffeine can speed up your dog's heart rate and can cause him to go into fatal convulsions. This means no coffee, tea, chocolate (see #1), or other foods and drinks with caffeine.

6. Drugs

Even over-the-counter drugs like ibuprofen, aspirin, and acetaminophen can be deadly for your dog. Fido shouldn't take any drugs not prescribed to him by his vet.

7. Animal bones (especially chicken and pork)

What's a dog without a bone? Safe, say veterinarians. Dogs love to chew on real bones, but most bones will split and splinter, and those pieces can get stuck in your dog's throat. Better to buy him a chew toy or flavored dog treat shaped like a bone.

8. Fatty foods

Like humans, dog love fatty foods, but (also like humans) these aren't the best things for them to eat. Dogs who consume excessively fatty foods (like bacon, turkey, or anything deep-fried) can contract pancreatitis.

9. Pitted fruits

The seeds of apples, peaches, pears, cherries, and other pitted fruits contain glucosides, a chemical that can cause cyanide poisoning, convulsions, and trouble breathing.

10. Raw meat

As more people have begun feeding their dogs raw food diets (trying to replicate the types of food wild wolves eat), parasites and other organisms have infected more dogs. Anything from salmon to beef can harbor parasites, so if you choose to feed your dog human food (instead of dog food), it's best to cook it first.

* * *

Dobermann's Dogs

Karl Friedrich Louis Dobermann was a 19th-century German tax collector who needed a strong dog to protect him while he traveled around the country collecting money. He created his own breed by mixing Rottweilers, Great Danes, German shepherds, and others. When he died in 1894, the Germans named the dog breed after him.

Vive les Chiens!

If dogs ruled the world, we'd likely all be
speaking French. Oui, c'est vrai!

The French love their dogs, and many French men and women spare no expense to ensure the comfort of their canine companions. Fresh meals prepared at the butcher shop, appointments at the doggy hairdresser, and overnight stays at a hotel (never say "kennel"!) are common enough occurrences in France that they don't raise any eyebrows. Dogs accompany their owners everywhere—to cafés, restaurants, movie theaters, and stores. Often, the canines are welcomed by an establishment's employees despite posted rules saying that dogs are not allowed. In fact, so ingrained is acceptance of dogs in French culture that when laws limiting canine freedom are passed, the statutes are usually ignored.

La Merde

However, there's a battle brewing over the . . . ahem . . . "surprises" all those pooches leave behind on city sidewalks. Whether in Paris, Toulouse, Nice, or Lyon, residents and visitors need to be mindful of where they step. *La merde*—translated literally, it means "the stink"—has caught numerous distracted pedestrians unaware and causes about 600 injuries each year to people who have slipped in the stuff.

Why do so many French dog owners allow their pooches to do their business right on the sidewalk? Because it most places, the poop is cleaned up by city employees who drive *caninettes*: large, green vacuum-scooters built to pick up the dog doo. In 2003, Paris, which spends more than $8.5 million annually to employ a team of 70 caninettes, tried to reduce costs by enacting a law requiring dog owners to clean up after their pets. At first, the law wasn't strictly enforced, but the poop problem finally became so bad that city residents held public demonstrations to bring attention to the issue. The law has finally started to make some headway thanks to fines ranging from 200 to 400 euros (about $267 to $535) for folks who don't pick up after their dogs.

Rover on the Rise . . . or Fall?

All of this legislation is having an effect on the Parisian dog population. By one estimate, the number of dogs in Paris dropped by more than 20 percent between 2002 to 2006 (from 190,000 to 147,000).

Part of this population decline has been attributed to the enforcement of dog laws, which also restrict where dogs are and aren't allowed due to health regulations. But don't think that all this means the French are losing their love for dogs. *Au contraire.* Although the number of dogs in Paris is on the decline, one can still enter a café or clothing boutique and find a small dog discreetly napping under a tablecloth, behind a curtain, or curled up inside an oversized handbag. And despite the new laws, many shop owners won't turn away patrons with dogs— some fear losing customers, but others are just dog fanciers themselves. As more laws pass that restrict where dogs can go and what their owners must do, the leash on French dogs may be tightening. But a love affair is a hard habit to break, so we'll probably see those Parisian dogs in restaurants and shops for many years to come.

* * *

The Bernards' Changing Face

Saint Bernards were originally bred at a monastery in the Swiss Alps, but an avalanche in the 19th century leveled the building and wiped out most of the original breeding stock. As a result, modern Saint Bernards are larger and less skilled at tracking and rescuing than the original animals because they had to be crossbred with other dogs to increase their numbers.

That's a Record

*Dogs do exceptional things,
but some are just amazing.*

Cinderella (Cindy) May A Holly Grey
Record: Highest jump

On October 3, 2003, Cindy (a greyhound from Florida) jumped her way into the record books when she leaped 5½ feet at Purina Dog Chow's Incredible Dog Challenge Show.

Duke
Record: Best climb

Duke, a seven-year-old Border collie/Australian shepherd mix from North Dakota, was inducted into the *Guinness World Records* book in 1998 after he climbed 13 tires stacked more than nine feet high and fetched a toy placed at the top. (As a reward for his effort, Duke was retired from cattle-dog duty at his owners' ranch.)

Danka Kordak Slovakia
Record: Smallest living dog

Danka, a long-haired Chihuahua, is the world's all-around smallest living dog. The pint-sized pup measured 5.4 inches tall and 7.4 inches long in May 2004—making her about the size of a soda bottle. (In terms of length, the smallest living dog is Heaven Sent Brandy, another female Chihuahua, who measured only six inches from her nose to the tip of her tail in January 2005.)

The smallest dog ever was a Yorkshire terrier who died in 1945. The unnamed pooch stood only 2.5 inches tall at the shoulder, measured 3.5 inches from the tip of his nose to the base of his tail, and weighed just four ounces.

Gibson
Record: Tallest living dog

Gibson, a mammoth Great Dane from California, stands more than 3½ feet tall at the shoulder.

Tigger
Record: Longest ears

Tigger, a bloodhound from Illinois, totes the world's longest dog ears: his right ear is 13.75 inches long, and the left ear is 13.5 inches.

Anastasia
Record: Popping the most balloons

This Jack Russell terrier can pop 100 balloons in 53.7 seconds, the fastest time recorded for a dog. Although Anastasia usually prefers to bite the balloons in the air, the record was set with the balloons tethered to the ground.

Brandy

Record: Longest tongue

Brandy, a seven-year-old boxer, had a 17-inch tongue. According to her owner, John Scheid, "her tongue was already adult-like at birth . . . at first we thought she would just grow into it, but as she grew her tongue also did."

Bluey

Record: Oldest dog

An Australian cattle dog named Bluey, who was owned by Les Hall of Victoria, Australia, was born in 1910 and wrangled Hall's cattle and sheep for nearly 20 years. When Bluey died on November 14, 1939, he was 29 years and 5 months old.

Striker

Record: Fastest at opening a car window

Using his paw and nose, Striker, a Border Collie who was owned and trained by Francis Gadassi of Hungary, recorded the fastest time in which a dog has unwound a nonelectric car window: 11.34 seconds . . . using just his paw and nose.

Augie

Record: Most tennis balls held in the mouth

On July 6, 2003, Augie, a golden retriever from Dallas, Texas, accomplished this feat, holding five regulation-size tennis balls in his mouth at one time.

More Dog Food
for Thought

Dog lovers' wisdom continues.

"I wonder if other dogs think poodles are members of a weird religious cult."

—*Rita Rudner*

"Outside of a dog, a man's best friend is a book. Inside of a dog, it is very dark."

—*Groucho Marx*

"There is no psychiatrist in the world like a puppy licking your face."

—*Ben Williams, dog breeder*

"Dogs' lives are too short. Their only fault, really."

—*Agnes Sligh Turnbull, writer*

"Anybody who doesn't know what soap tastes like never washed a dog."

—*Franklin P. Jones, writer*

"My dog is half pit bull, half poodle. Not much of a guard dog, but a vicious gossip."

—*Craig Shoemaker, comedian*

"Dogs need to sniff the ground; it's how they keep abreast of current events. The ground is a giant dog newspaper, containing all kinds of late-breaking dog news items."

—*Dave Barry*

"Some days, you're the dog; some days, you're the hydrant."

—*Anonymous*

"People who keep dogs are cowards who haven't got the guts to bite people themselves."

—*August Strindberg, playwright*

"A dog is the only thing on this earth that loves you more than he loves himself."

—*Anonymous*

"When a man's best friend is his dog, that dog has a problem."

—*Edward Abbey, environmentalist*

"If dogs could talk, perhaps we would find it as hard to get along with them as we do with people."

—*Karel Capek, writer*

"The average dog is a nicer person than the average person."

—*Andy Rooney*

The Dog Whisperer

*When it comes to training canines, no one knows better than
Cesar Millan that it's a dog-eat-dog world out there.*

Techniques Born on the Farm

Millan's approach to training dogs is based in large part on
his own experiences as a child in Mexico. His grandfather
worked on a farm near the western town of Ixpalino.
There, Millan first saw what he calls dogs' "pack behavior"
and how it was affected by the leadership—or lack of it—
of the humans in charge of the dogs. He also observed that
the dogs on the farm did the jobs that needed doing without special training or being coaxed with treats. Millan
believed that the calm, assertive way his grandfather led
his animals affected this positive behavior.

Coming to America

At the age of 15, Millan got a job working with a veterinarian in Mazatlan. He had a special touch with dogs and
was able to calm even the most poorly behaved animals.
These skills impressed his bosses, but local kids nicknamed
him "El Perrero," or the "Dog Boy." The nickname wasn't
flattering—in Mexico, dogs were considered dirty and
wild—but the name and Millan's love of dogs stuck.

About six years later, in 1990, 21-year-old Millan moved to California. He held many jobs; one was as a dog groomer, and as other animal handlers watched Millan manage aggressive dogs, they were impressed. Soon, word of his talents spread throughout Los Angeles. Actors Will and Jada Pinkett Smith were among the first to seek Millan's help for their own cantankerous canines. They were so happy with his techniques that they recommended Millan to their friends. Before long, he had a list of celebrity clients and had opened a dog school in L.A., Pacific Point Canine Academy. In 2004, he put his techniques to work on the National Geographic Channel's *Dog Whisperer*, and in 2006, he published a book called *Cesar's Way*.

At the Head of the Pack

Millan believes that embracing your dog's desire to be part of a pack, with you as the head honcho, can change even the most difficult canine into a pleasant pooch. He argues that in a healthy pack, dogs learn rules, boundaries, and limitations. Millan himself has numerous dogs (sometimes as many as 50) at his home, all unchained, living harmoniously and under control. He believes that, because dogs think more in terms of energy than actual behavior, the energy that owners project toward their pets governs the relationship. So Millan suggests that owners act like mother dogs who uses natural canine techniques to keep her pups in line if they misbehave. He uses the "alpha roll," flipping a dog on its back and holding the animal in that position to emphasize domination. He also suggests walking dogs several times a day with the owner at the front of the pack and the dogs in the rear, as opposed to walking with the animal in front.

Even with all his successes, Millan's techniques are controversial: some animal advocates believe he's too aggressive and heavy-handed. The critics also deride his lack of formal training. But Millan shrugs off his detractors, saying, "I'm bringing back common sense, as far as I'm concerned. There are millions of dogs in America, and they need help. I'm helping them . . . my goal is always a calm, assertive human and a calm, submissive dog."

* * *

Chomp, Chomp

Mail carriers hoping to avoid biting dogs are safest in New York City; no carriers were attacked by dogs there in 2006. At the other end of the scale, 96 mail carriers were bitten in Santa Ana, California, in 2006.

Superstitious Pups

Dogs are generally considered mankind's most consistent and selfless friend, but they're also the subject of some interesting superstitions.

- Fishermen traditionally regard dogs as unlucky and will not allow one to accompany them in a boat. It is bad form to mention the word "dog" while at sea.

- Having a dog present while playing cards is said to cause arguments among the players.

- In Scotland, people believe that a strange dog at the door foretells a new friendship.

- In England, meeting a black-and-white or spotted dog on the way to a business appointment is said to bring good luck.

- The Irish believe that if a dog howls near the house of a sick person, it's a sign that the patient will not recover. The Egyptians, Hebrews, Greeks, and Romans also took a dog's howling as an ominous sign. The Romans even noted a howling dog among the omens that preceded the death of Caesar.

- The ancient Greeks believed that dogs could sense supernatural beings such as ghosts, spirits, fairies, or other entities invisible to human eyes. Barking, whimpering, or howling was the way a dog warned humans of supernatural occurrences.

- Ancient Persians thought that dogs could protect a dying soul from possession by evil spirits. So when death was imminent, the Persians brought a dog to the sick person's bedside to drive away the negative spirits that might attack his newly released soul.

* * *

Splish Splash

Since 2004, Splash Dogs, a Northern California group, has organized dock jumping competitions all over the western United States. The goal: to see whose dog can jump the farthest into a pool of water. The top prize is $500, and the current Splash Dogs record is 26.5 feet, set by a retriever named Henry.

More Remarkable Reunions

On page 91, we told you about three dogs who overcame incredible odds to return home. Here are three more.

Fluffy: Look Out Below!

In July 2005, Fluffy, a two-year-old bichon frise, escaped from the fenced backyard of his home in Ontario, Canada. His owners, Glenn and Marla Lyons, began an immediate search, but they had no luck until they contacted the local branch of the Society for the Prevention of Cruelty to Animals. The SPCA didn't have the dog at its shelter, but the folks there had gotten a call from someone who'd seen a little white dog being swept down the Niagara River. The Lyons knew it had to be Fluffy and that it was very bad news. That stretch of the river, just 12 miles above Niagara Falls, had taken the lives of many swimmers, and no one believed that a 10-pound dog could survive it. The family waited for more news.

That afternoon, they got it. A fisherman on Niagara's American side pulled Fluffy out of the river and brought the dog the SPCA in Buffalo, which immediately contacted the branch across the river. The little dog was soaked and tired, but he'd survived the swift currents and undertows. Pooch and owners were reunited, and we have a hunch that Fluffy now stays in his yard.

Candi: On the Lam

In October 2006, Candi, a sheltie from New Brunswick, Canada, got spooked in her backyard by an excavation team that was digging a well and took off. Her owner did everything she could to find Candi, but the dog seemed to prefer her newfound freedom and managed to evade even the most persistent rescuers. She pulled off her collar and left it behind. When she got caught in a river current and a man pulled her to safety, she ran away before he could get a firm hold on her. Neighbors left food out for her, which she ate, but she didn't hang around. Snowshoers tried to trail her, but they never caught sight of her.

Finally, the next spring, Candi seemed to have had enough of the big bad world and wandered into her backyard where her owner caught her. Today, Candi's still at home, but she's no longer allowed to go outside alone.

Justice: In the Wake of Katrina

When the helicopter landed on the apartment building of the Lafitte housing development in New Orleans' flooded Sixth Ward a week after Hurricane Katrina, Marion Stevenson helped to pull all but one of her family members to safety. Justice, her 10-year-old black Lab mix, had to stay behind. The dog survived alone in the flooded apartment building for two more weeks before she was finally rescued and placed in a makeshift dog shelter in a nearby Winn-Dixie parking lot. From there, she moved to the Roycefield Kennel in Hillsborough, New Jersey, where she was assigned a case number and her picture was placed on a Web site devoted to reuniting owners with pets lost in the flooding.

More than 1,000 miles away in Houma, Louisiana, Marion Stevenson was staying with her father and checking in with the Humane Society daily, just in case someone had found Justice. Several weeks passed before she had any news, but one night, after hours of searching online for clues to her dog's whereabouts, Stevenson saw it—there was Justice's picture! The Humane Society helped Stevenson get in touch with the people at the Roycefield Kennel. With a little finagling, Justice came home just in time for Thanksgiving.

* * *

"To a dog, every man is Napoléon; hence the constant popularity of dogs."

—*Aldous Huxley, writer*

First Aid for Fido

*The ASPCA and American Kennel Club have some advice
for those tense minutes after your pup has been injured.*

Get to the Vet

If your dog is injured, the first priority is to get him to the
vet as quickly as possible.

Muzzle Your Dog

Even if your dog has always been trustworthy, if he's been
injured and is in pain, his first instinct will be to bite, so
you should restrain him with a muzzle. Be sure not to let
the muzzle constrict his breathing, and never use a muzzle
on a dog who is vomiting or having trouble breathing.

Build a Makeshift Stretcher

If your dog has a broken limb or can't stand up on his
own, create a makeshift stretcher from a particle board, an
old blanket, or a large towel for his trip to the veterinarian—take special care not to move his spine or head. Grab
the nape of his neck and the skin on his back, gently drag
him onto the stretcher, and call the vet on your way there
so the staff can be prepared to handle the emergency.

Apply Pressure to Any Bleeding

To stop external bleeding, use gauze or even a clean hand to apply pressure evenly to the affected area. For heavy bleeding, hold the pressure steady for 10 minutes.

Administer CPR

Cardiopulmonary respiration can be a lifesaver for anyone, even dogs. To perform doggy CPR, keep your pooch on his side and open his mouth to check for obstructions. Cover his nose with your mouth and exhale gently. Repeat with 10 to 12 breaths per minute. Massage the dog's heart only if it stops beating. To do this, keep the dog in the same position you used for the breathing, and place your hands over his heart on the left side. Press down about 70 times per minute.

Please note: The above techniques are general information only and should be used with caution. It is most advisable to attend a basic course on pet first aid or talk to your pet's veterinarian about all lifesaving techniques.

* * *

Purrrrfect

Not all of your dog's throaty vocalizations are meant to express fear or frustration. Sometimes, dogs convey happiness by making a growl-like sound similar to a cat's purr.

Nuts About Mutts

*If you're looking for a companion dog, mixed breeds,
better known as mutts, are the way to go. Here's why.*

A Good Investment

From a financial viewpoint, mutts are a bargain. The purchase price for purebred pooches ranges from hundreds to thousands of dollars, but mutts from a local animal shelter are usually available for $100 or less. Sometimes, they're even free. Also, according to the National Humane Society, fees for pets adopted from local animal shelters usually include vaccinations, deworming, and spaying or neutering, things that aren't typically included when you buy a purebred dog. That means less money spent at the vet when you bring your new pet home.

Problem-Free Pets

Purebred dogs can have a myriad of health problems. Veterinarians have documented as many as 300 genetic health defects among the breeds. These include disorders of the cardiovascular system, skin and eye conditions, immuno-logic disorders, and nervous system disorders. Breeding the same champion dogs over and over limits the gene pool and increases the chances of defective genes becoming common in the breed. Because mutts have parents of different breeds, they have a more varied gene pool and less chance for genetic defects.

A Mutt by Any Other Name

Although they're best known as mutts, mixed-breed dogs have earned a variety of nicknames in different cultures around the world.

- United States: Heinz 57. This is a playful reference to the popular steak sauce's "57 varieties," though there are hundreds of kinds of mutts.
- United Kingdom: mongrels
- Hawaii: poi dogs, and in the Bahamas, "pot cakes." Both reference strays' diet of garbage or table scraps.
- Brazil and the Dominican Republic: *Vira-lata*, because strays have a reputation of scrounging through trash-cans looking for food. (In Spanish, *vira* means "to turn," or "to bring down, " and *lata* means "trash can.")

* * *

More than 1 million U.S. dog owners have designated their dogs as the primary beneficiary in their wills.

Jokes on Us

*Moan, groan, and chuckle at some
of our favorite silly dog jokes.*

What did the dog say when he sat on sandpaper?
Rough!

What do you get if you cross a sheepdog with a
rose?
A collie-flower

What is a dog's favorite city?
New Yorkie

Who is a dog's favorite comedian?
Growlcho Marx

What breed of dog loves to take baths?
A shampoodle

What kind of dog does Dracula have?
A bloodhound

Where should you never take a dog?
The flea market

Classic Cartoon Canines

*Anyone who was a child between 1960 and 1980
is bound to remember these animated pooches who helped
make syndicated cartoons an American staple.*

Fido of the Future

On the heels of *The Flintstones*—the first successful prime-
time animated series—cartoon pioneers Joseph Barbera
and William Hanna imagined another animated world,
this one set sometime in the 21st century. *The Jetsons*
debuted in September 1962 and ran every Sunday night
until March 1963. The creators shot only 24 episodes of
that original series (the series reappeared with new
episodes in the 1980s), but they reran them on Saturday
mornings for decades. Set in sky-high Orbit City, the show
featured the family of George Jetson—his wife Jane;
daughter Judy; son Elroy; and . . .

In the fifth episode, Elroy found Astro, a bumbling gray-
and-white hound who followed the boy home from school.
Elroy, Jane, and Judy wanted to keep the dog, but George
didn't want the responsibilities of a new pet. At first,
George bought his family a state-of-the-art, apartment-
approved, robot-pet named Lectronimo, but when the Cat
Burglar, a masked marauder prowling Orbit City, broke
into the family's apartment, the electronic canine couldn't

seem to catch the burglar. In the end, Astro proved himself and earned a spot in the family by colliding with the real burglar and saving the day.

Despite these heroics, Astro was a cowardly canine best known for his good intentions and desire to please. Ultimately, he caused more trouble for his master than good. He also had several signature phrases, including "Ruh-Roh" and "Right, Reorge," which were voiced by actor Don Messick, who also provided the voices of Scooby-Doo, Bamm-Bamm Rubble, and Papa Smurf.

Did You Know? In *The Jetsons*' 15th episode, Astro is revealed to be a dog named Tralfaz, the long-lost pet of zillionaire tycoon J. P. Gottrockets. The bigwig takes the family to court and wins custody of the canine but later has a change of heart. He returns Astro to the Jetsons when he sees how happy they make the pup.

Slow and Steady

Ace animator Tex Avery, who helped create such enduring cartoon characters as Daffy Duck and Bugs Bunny, also held the pen behind a white basset hound called Droopy Dog. This pooch first hit the silver screen in 1943 in an animated MGM short called *Dumb-Hounded*, but he wasn't called "Droopy" until 1945's *The Shooting of Dan McGoo*. Although Droopy was a low-key pooch whose speech and movements dragged . . . well . . . droopily, he could always outwit and defeat his adversaries, including

Butch the bulldog and an unnamed villainous wolf. Droopy's big-screen days came to an end in the late 1950s when MGM shut down its animation studio. But he found new life in the 1970s in a series of television shorts; in the 1980s as an elevator operator in the film *Who Framed Roger Rabbit?*; and in the 1990s as a character on *Tom & Jerry*.

Did You Know? Droopy earned an Oscar nomination in 1957 for *One Droopy Knight* but ultimately lost to *Birds Anonymous*, a spoof on Alcoholics Anonymous in which Sylvester (of Sylvester and Tweety fame) went through the 12-step process to deal with his bird-eating addiction.

The Law-Dawg

Originally a Terrytoons cartoon character, Deputy Dawg appeared on television in CBS cartoons from 1959 to 1972. He was a bumbling sheriff's deputy who was stationed in Mississippi's rural bayous, where he passed the time with his pals Muskie the Muskrat and Vincent Van Gopher. Deputy spent most of his days fishing and chasing Muskie and Vincent out of vegetable patches. Dayton Allen, who played the magpies Heckle and Jeckle and many other Terrytoons characters, provided Deputy's voice.

Did You Know? Actor Jim Carrey calls Deputy Dawg his favorite cartoon character.

Martial Artist Extraordinaire

Hong Kong Phooey, a martial-arts superdog (and a spoof on 1970s kung fu heroes), was the alter ego of mild-mannered Penrod "Penry" Pooch. As long as there was no trouble on the horizon, Penry spent his days working as a police station janitor. But when villainous characters appeared, Penry dove into a filing cabinet, changed into his orange karate outfit and black eye mask, and emerged as Hong Kong Phooey, super crime-fighter. His superhero mobile, called the Phooeymobile, became whatever kind of transportation he needed with just a "bonging of the gong," and he was usually accompanied by his striped cat, Spot.

Hong Kong Phooey, yet another Hanna-Barbera cartoon, originally aired on Saturday mornings in 1974; it lived on in syndication for many years after that. Scatman Crothers gave Phooey his voice. (He also played Scat Cat in Disney's *The Aristocats*.)

Did You Know? Penrod Pooch learned his martial arts skills through a correspondence course, and during battles with bad guys, he often consulted his textbook, *The Hong Kong Book of Kung Fu*.

The Blue Dog with a Heart of Gold

In 1958, Hanna and Barbera premiered their first animated series made strictly for TV. *The Huckleberry Hound Show* ran on Thursday afternoons in most markets and told the story of Huckleberry, a kind-hearted, honest, hard-working blue dog trying out a variety of careers. In the pilot episode, "Wee Willie," he played a policeman who took on the job of returning an escaped gorilla to the zoo. In later episodes, Huckleberry dabbled in such professions as mailman, lion tamer, veterinarian, explorer, firefighter, and even dogcatcher.

Voice actor Daws Butler (the original Elroy on *The Jetsons*) provided Huckleberry's Southern drawl. The voice was inspired, at least in part, by a neighbor of Daws' wife, though many people recognized similarities between Huckleberry and then-film actor Andy Griffith. Daws also used the voice for Droopy Dog's wolf foe.

Did You Know? Hanna-Barbera made 55 *Huckleberry Hound* episodes during the show's four years on the air. (Like most cartoon series, it lived on much longer in syndication.) In 1960, the show won an Emmy Award—the first ever presented to an animated series.

* * *

All Bite and No Bark

The basenji, a type of hunting dog originally from Africa, is the only canine breed that doesn't bark . . . not like other dogs, anyway. Basenjis do make noise: they yelp, yodel, and even make a scream-like barking sound. But their larynxes are positioned differently than most dogs', which makes traditional barking impossible for them.

Monumental
Achievements

*Courageous canines have been immortalized in statues
all over the world. Here are some of our favorites.*

Statue of Mancs

Where: Miskolc, Hungary

Details: Mancs (which means "paw" in Hungarian) was a German shepherd rescue dog with a special talent for finding earthquake survivors beneath rubble. He could tell, just by smelling, if a person were dead or alive. If the person was dead, Mancs lay down. If the person was alive, he stood up, wagged his tail, and barked. Mancs died in 2006 of a pulmonary embolism; he was 13.

Statue's Status: Unveiled in 2004

Dog on the Tuckerbox

Where: Australia

Details: This statue, located at Snake Gully in Australia, is a tribute to the country's pioneers. According to one version of the folk tale, "Dog on the Tuckerbox" was a pet who loyally guarded his owner's tuckerbox (lunch box) while the man went off to find someone to help him free a team of oxen that had gotten stuck in a river. The owner never returned, but the dog continued to guard the tucker-box until he died himself. Sixty years later, in 1992, the residents of Snake Gully began hosting an annual "Dog on the Tuckerbox" festival every November. The festival includes a horse race called the Snake Gully Cup, which has more than $100,000 in prize money. The festival also includes a sportsman's dinner and showcases local crafts and cooking.

Statue's Status: Unveiled in 1932

United States War Dog Memorial

Where: Holmdel, New Jersey

Details: A life-size bronze statue of a soldier and his German shepherd decorates the grounds of the New Jersey Vietnam Veterans Memorial. The statue cost $100,000 and took seven years to make. It recognizes the role of dogs in American wars, including World War II, Korea, and Vietnam.

Statue's Status: Unveiled on June 10, 2006

Bum

Where: San Diego, California

Details: Bum was a Saint Bernard/spaniel mix who arrived in San Diego in 1886 as a steamship stowaway. He was so friendly that restaurant owners, saloon patrons, and street-car riders all welcomed him. When a dogcatcher tried to capture Bum, San Diegans intervened and got him released so that he was free to roam the streets again. To

prevent him from being caught a second time, city officials created San Diego's first dog license and put Bum's picture on it so that everyone would know who he was. The dog also impressed locals with his heroics: legend has it that Bum lost one of his front legs when he was hit by a train while saving a puppy who'd gotten stuck on the tracks.
Statue's Status: As of 2007, Bum's statue was in the planning stages.

California Police Canine Memorial
Where: Davis, California
Details: Located on the grounds of the Davis School of Veterinary Medicine, this life-size bronze statue of a German shepherd on a seven-pointed black granite star is dedicated to police dogs killed in the line of duty.
Statue's Status: Unveiled on October 2, 2002

To read about more dog heroes,
turn to pages 122.

* * *

Myth-conception

Myth: Dogs sweat through their panting tongues.
Fact: Panting helps them cool off, but they sweat through their feet.

199

Fleas Be Gone!

Fleas have been around for more than 160 million years. It seems that nothing—mass extinctions, climate changes, industrialization, you name it—can defeat the nasty little critters. Why should all the flea-control products for dogs be any different?

Early Flea Control

In the mid-20th century, new advances were made in the field of veterinary science, especially in the area of dog and cat health. This can be attributed, in part, to the growth of the automobile industry and rapid urbanization, which made people less dependent on horses and farm life. Many of the vets who had specialized in treating horses and other farm animals shifted their focus to smaller household pets, which were growing in popularity. And tackling the flea problem became a priority because, as people moved to cities and lived in close quarters with their pets, the tiny insects became a nuisance. Other than diligent cleanliness, though, few flea-control options were available. One of the earliest "treatments" was bathing the dog in motor oil. This killed any fleas in the animals' coat but also could make the dogs sick when they licked the oil off their bodies.

Death to Fleas!

In 1964, Dr. Robert Goulding Jr. of Oregon State University invented slow-release pesticides. By applying the poison to a plastic strip, Goulding created the first flea collar, which became a fixture on many dogs' necks for the rest of the century. Although the flea collar was effective in killing fleas, it had a few drawbacks. For one thing, it killed only the fleas that ventured too close to the collar—fleas could camp out on the dog's back and hind legs and not be concerned about the toxic fumes lingering near his neck. Also, dogs with sensitive skin sometimes had adverse reactions to the chemicals in the collars, resulting in skin inflammation. Other pets in the household could be affected as well: permethrin, a common insecticide used in flea collars, can be fatal to cats in high doses.

The flea collar is not completely useless, however. Adding one to a vacuum-cleaner bag is an excellent way to ensure that any fleas picked up by the vacuum are killed before they can escape. (What about those fancy ultrasonic flea collars? Given the fact that fleas cannot detect sound waves, it doesn't take much to figure out that those products are more of a marketing gimmick than a scientifically sound solution to the flea problem.)

Sniffing, Not Scratching

Flea dips and shampoos, while effective, need to be used frequently. Many flea dips contain substances, either natural or chemical, that alter your pet's odor and make fleas unable to locate him by smell, which is the flea's primary means of finding a host. If used too often, though, these products can can dry out a dog's skin. Many alternative holistic dips and shampoos are available today. Most of these contain aromatic oils such as lemon, neem, karanja, and eucalyptus, all of which are designed to make your dog smell, well . . . undogly. Other holistic remedies include brewer's yeast and garlic tablets. B vitamins are also supposed to repel fleas, but no scientific studies to date support this claim. Pennyroyal oil is another holistic option, but this substance can be toxic to dogs in high doses—it can cause paralysis, seizures, and liver problems.

A Dirty Solution

Diatomaceous earth is a popular flea-control powder made of crushed diatomite rock, which is formed by fossilized sea algae. It's used primarily outside the house—in garden beds, lawns, and cracks and crevices where insects like to nest—but it can also be used under heavy furniture and in other out-of-the way places. Diatomaceous earth is a fine powder that is absorbed by the waxy coating of a flea's body; it causes the flea to become dehydrated and unable to reproduce. People who apply the powder should always wear a dust mask to avoid inhaling it. Once it's applied, though, diatomaceous earth is generally harmless to pets and humans and is a good option for controlling fleas.

An Enduring Insect

The advent of flea-control medications in the 1990s ushered in a new era. Dog owners could now give their pet a monthly tablet or spot-on application that killed not only adult fleas but thousands of unhatched eggs as well. Some of these medications kill the fleas (and sometimes the eggs, too) by direct contact, whereas others require that the flea bite the dog and draw blood. Many veterinarians now prescribe these medications because they've proven to be effective. Concerns over possible long-term risks to pets' health, though, have led a growing number of dog owners to seek out alternative treatments, including fragrant oils, wood shavings, and the aforementioned brewer's yeast and garlic. No matter the method, though, fleas just won't go away for good. Millions of years after humans and dogs have disappeared from the earth, fleas are likely to still be around . . . as long as there is blood to be enjoyed.

Why So Blue?

Inspired by a local legend, artist George Rodrigue created the Absolut Vodka Blue Dog in 1984.

Born on the Bayou

George Rodrigue was born in 1944 in the southern Louisiana town of New Iberia, a place that is best known for Tabasco factories and rock salt. As an eight-year-old, Rodrigue started painting and sculpting while recovering from polio. Later, he studied with private teachers before attending the University of Southwestern Louisiana (now the University of Louisiana at Lafyette) and Los Angeles' Art Center College of Design. Although Rodrigue considered moving to New York City to find work as an artist, Louisiana called him home. He returned to the state in 1967 and took a job as art director for an advertising agency.

Rodrigue continued to find inspiration in the culture that surrounded him. His first major work was called *The Aioli Dinner*. It featured a meeting of New Iberia's Aioli Gourmet Dinner Club, a men's-only club that gathered at various homes in New Iberia for conversation and a good meal. The painting was first displayed at the Iberia Parish Library in 1971; today, it hangs in the New Orleans Museum of Art.

The Blue Loup-Garou

Another inspiration was a local legend that tells of a
mythical werewolf called the loup-garou, a creature different from the typical Hollywood werewolf. The loup-garou
isn't created when a werewolf bites someone; instead, anyone who commits a heinous sin might turn into a loup-
garou. Says Louisiana storyteller John Verret, "You do
something wrong . . . then . . . God turn his back on you.
Then the devil takes over."

The frightening moral legend stuck in Rodrigue's
head. In the early 1980s, when he was asked to design
the cover of a book of Louisiana ghost stories, his creative mind returned to the cursed loup-garou. He wasn't
sure, though, exactly what the animal should look like.
It wasn't until he discovered some photos of his own dog
Tiffany, who had passed away several years before, that
he settled on an idea. His creature was a pale blue
spaniel/terrier with wide black-and-white eyes. She
stood in front of a red manor house and beneath a blue-
gray night sky . . . waiting.

Rodrigue christened his creation the "Blue Dog" and
enjoyed it so much that he continued to improve it over
the next few years. The dog's eyes changed to yellow, and
she appeared in new settings: in a cemetery or next to a
bayou. The dog also took on a friendlier, less ominous
tone, looking more like a wide-eyed companion than a
cursed creature.

Absolut Success

Rodrigue wasn't the only one who liked the Blue Dog. The Absolut Vodka company enjoyed her so much that in 1992, the company named Rodrigue as one of its Absolut Artists, an elite group that included Andy Warhol. Absolut also used the Blue Dog in its ad campaigns: Rodrigue painted the pooch in a colorful, though abstract, living room in front of a bouquet of flowers blooming from an Absolut bottle.

The Disaster

Over the next 15 years, Rodrigue continued to paint the Blue Dog; the animal appeared in several calendars and books. But in 2005, she was back in the spotlight; the Blue Dog appeared in a painting called *We Will Rise Again,* which benefited the Red Cross in the wake of Hurricane Katrina.

Rodrigue knew the disaster firsthand—his home and New Orleans gallery were damaged in the hurricane. In the painting, the Blue Dog sits in front of an American flag; both are submerged. The dog's eyes are red, and she has a red cross on her chest. The painting was one in a series that Rodrigue created after the flooding; others were called *Throw Me Something FEMA* and *You Can't Drown the Blues.* The sale of these paintings benefited Blue Dog Relief, an organization Rodrigue started in 2006. To date, it has raised more than $1 million.

Dog Tales, Part 2

On page 103, we introduced you to some
mythological dogs. Here are two more.

Fenrir (also called Fenrisulfr)

This enormous wolf appears in Scandinavian mythology as
the offspring of Loki (the Norse god of mischief) and
Angrboda (a giantess). Fenrir's destiny, as prophesized in a
Norse creation poem, was to devour the chief god Odin
during the battle at the end of the world. When Odin
found out about the prophesy, he brought Fenrir to live
among the gods, who chained him, blinded him, and tried
to trick him. Fenrir wouldn't fall for their tricks, though,
and ultimately bit off one of the god's hands. The gods
then chained Fenrir to a rock one mile underground.
Legend holds that when the mythic battle (called
Ragnarök) at the end of the world begins, Fenrir will break
free from his bonds and join the battle against the gods.
The Scandinavians are still waiting.

Quick Fact: One of the characters in the Harry Potter series
was named after this wolf. Fenrir Greyback is introduced in
Harry Potter and the Half-Blood Prince as a scary dark wizard
who attacks children and turns them into werewolves.

Pan Gu

The southern Chinese offer a version of a common Chinese creation myth that says the Chinese creator god, Pan Gu, is half man and half dog. In this legend, Pan Gu was the dog of the earth god, King Gao Xin, whose biggest rival was another god named King Fang. King Gao offered his daughter's hand in marriage to anyone who could kill his adversary. Everyone was afraid of King Fang except Pan Gu, who went to the king's palace and ingratiated himself to his master's rival god.

Thinking that Pan Gu had abandoned his master, King Fang welcomed the dog and organized a banquet for him. But that evening, Pan Gu attacked King Fang and bit off his head. The dog returned to King Gao's palace with the head, and King Gao was thrilled and rewarded Pan Gu with a heaping plate of meat. But the dog wasn't interested. He wanted the princess and fell into a depression when he realized King Gao wouldn't let a dog marry his daughter.

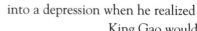

Fortunately, the lovers had an idea: The king had a magic golden bell that could turn the dog into a man.

If Pan Gu stayed beneath the bell and hid for seven days, he'd become human and be able to marry the princess.

All went well until the sixth day, when the impatient princess peeked under the bell and interrupted the transformation process, leaving Pan Gu with the head of a dog and the body of a man. King Gao thought that was enough, though, and allowed Pan Gu to marry the princess. The couple moved to Earth—taking up residence in the remote mountains of southern China—and lived happily ever after. Their children became the ancestors of mankind.

Quick Fact: Pan Gu is known as "King Pan" in southern China, where there are temples and pavilions built in his honor.

* * *

Duncan's Military Dogs

When World War II began, Lee Duncan—famous for training German shepherd actor Rin Tin Tin—wanted to serve but was unable due to an injury. Instead, he and Rin Tin Tin III became the head trainers at Camp Hahn, a training camp for military dogs. Together, they trained more than 5,000 dogs and handlers for the war effort.

A Breed Apart

*Dogs may be the among the oldest domesticated
animals, but they started out wild. Here's how eons
of human contact turned wolves into pets.*

A 12,000-year-old grave in Israel offers touching
evidence of the long, close relationship between
humans and dogs. The grave contains a human skeleton
whose hand rests on the bones of a puppy. Through the
centuries, dogs have given people loyalty, aid, and companionship. But how did people come to have such understanding and helpful friends?

Never Cry Wolf

Scientists have discovered 400,000-year-old wolf bones
mingled with human bones, but they think the man/wolf
relationship goes back even farther than that. Early
humans probably first used wolves as food, but the wolves
would also have been using humans, scavenging through
their garbage and over time moving closer to the centers
of camps and the humans' food source—the campfire.
After a while, humans accepted the gentler wolves as part
of the group.

Wolf packs and early human tribes also had a lot in
common. They were both willing to follow a leader, coop-

erate, and work together to protect members of their group. So wolf/human cooperation was natural—especially when it came to hunting.

Wolves started to follow humans when they went hunting and gave off cues when prey was around. The humans soon figured out that wolves possessed a superior sense of smell and could detect prey at long distances. Man and wolf began to cooperate, and eventually, wolves became active participants and true partners with humans in the hunt for food.

An Evolving Puppy Tale

When selecting a wolf pal, humans naturally favored the most cooperative animals. They associated cooperative behavior with a puppylike appearance in adult wolves and encouraged those animals to stick around. Humans also picked out the most gentle, trainable puppies to raise.

In effect, humans replaced nature's selection process with a man-made one. And after thousands of years of human meddling—about 14,000 years ago—a new animal evolved. Thanks to domestication and their diet, these animals had smaller brains, heads, and teeth than wild wolves. We call them dogs, and they became increasingly important to humans because of their usefulness and their companionship.

To Breed or Not to Breed

Dogs always had a variety of size and body proportions, but

about 3,000 to 4,000 years ago, unable to leave well enough alone, people tinkered with Mother Nature in earnest to create specialized working and companion dogs. That's when the different breeds really emerged.

As breeding continued, dogs became more specialized. Herding dogs were bred to work with livestock. Sporting dogs were bred for bird hunting. Hounds were bred to hunt by scent or by sight. Working dogs were bred to perform many tasks, including herding, hauling, and guarding. Terriers were bred to hunt rodents and other vermin. Toy breeds were bred to be companions or simply lap warmers.

Sweet Success

Dogs have been successful because they adapted well to the needs of humans for loyalty, companionship, and assistance. Dogs and people communicate effectively through voice, body language, and facial expressions . . . although in many ways, dogs seem better at understanding humans than humans are at understanding dogs.

Dogs and humans also have a relationship based on mutual support. Dogs have great difficulty surviving on their own, and a dog's dependence on humans makes him a sensitive friend.

* * *

Mark your calendar: August 26 is National Dog Day.

Just Good Sense

Canines have a leg up on humans in just about every "sense." Here's a look at dog eyes, ears, and noses and how they compare with our own.

Eyes

In comparing dog and human eyes, it's hard to say who has the greater ability. Humans can't compete against a dog's excellent peripheral vision—dogs have eyes that sit back along the sides of their heads at an outward angle, which gives them great peripheral vision. But humans have far better color vision. Dogs see mostly gray, black, and white. Any colors (usually red and green hues) are dull compared to the rich colors in the human perspective. But dogs can detect movement, even when it's slight, from great distances. After all, the first dogs needed to hunt, and for them to survive, seeing a bright red flower along the trail or a purple berry growing on a bush was much less important than catching sight of a rabbit's tail moving in the brush. When it comes to night vision, dogs are also far superior because they have a reflective tissue behind their retinas that concentrates light. So if you're wondering whether or not you should leave a night light on for Fido, don't bother. He can maneuver easily around the living room furniture in the dark.

Ears

Every dog owner can attest to how powerful a dog's hearing is. Canine ears perk up long before a doorbell chimes to announce a visitor. The actual mechanics of the dog's ear contributes to his excellent hearing. A dog's ears swivel to locate a sound, and the ears can move independently of each other. Both of these capabilities enable dogs to determine a sound's exact location very quickly. Dogs also hear at a wide range of frequencies and at much lower volumes than humans. A dog can hear clearly from a distance of 200 feet the muffled sounds that humans hear from 50 feet away.

Noses

A dog's superior hearing doesn't begin to compare to the strength of his nose, though. To get a perspective of how highly developed a dog's sense of smell is, consider this: Humans have 5 million olfactory cells in their noses that enable them to discern scents. Dogs have between 150 million and 250 million such cells in their significantly larger noses. And once all that information reaches the dogs' brains, they have 40 times more olfactory cells than humans do to process all the information. What does this mean? Experts say that a dog could detect a single drop of human sweat dissolved in 1 million quarts of water. And, once a dog has picked up the scent of a human or animal, he isn't likely to ever forget it. Even in a perfume factory or junkyard, the dog could pick out that unique scent.

First Friends

*Residents of the White House have long shared
their space with canine friends. Can you identify
the presidents who owned these dogs?*

1. The beagles Him and Her were owned by this presi-
dent, who caused a storm of protest when he lifted
"Him" up by his ears. (Hint: The dramatic event
unfolded in the 1960s.)
A. Lyndon B. Johnson
B. John F. Kennedy
C. Richard Nixon

2. A Scottish terrier named Fala was the canine companion of this longest-serving president, who made sure
that the White House staff included a bone for Fala
every morning with the president's breakfast tray.
A. Harry Truman
B. Jimmy Carter
C. Franklin D. Roosevelt

3. Fido belonged to this president before he was elected.
When it came time to move into the White House, the
mutt stayed behind in Springfield, entrusted to a pair of

neighborhood boys who promised never to scold Fido or tie him up alone in the backyard.

A. Dwight D. Eisenhower

B. Abraham Lincoln

C. Theodore Roosevelt

4. Spot, this president's English springer spaniel, was the daughter of a former presidential dog.

A. John F. Kennedy

B. Gerald Ford

C. George W. Bush

5. Rex, this president's King Charles spaniel, often dragged his master and mistress away from reporters and photographers by pulling hard on his leash. (Hint: The president has a economic policy named for him.)

A. Ronald Reagan

B. George H. W. Bush

C. Bill Clinton

6. This president, who served for most of the 1920s, had several dogs during his lifetime, including an Airedale named Paul Pry and a sheepdog named Calamity Jane.

A. Woodrow Wilson

B. Calvin Coolidge

C. Herbert Hoover

For answers, turn to page 227.

More Good Dogs

Rottweilers and pit bulls have a bad rep—they're called aggressive,
mean, ferocious, and angry. But these dogs are called "heroes."

Reona

What she did: During the 1989 San Francisco earthquake,
Reona, a Rottweiler from Watsonville, California, raced
into the house next door to save five-year-old Vivian
Cooper. Vivian had epilepsy, and the fear and excitement
related to the quake could have easily brought on a
seizure. But Reona comforted and protected the little girl.
The dog pushed Vivian against the kitchen cabinets as a
microwave oven crashed onto the floor where the child
had been standing, and Vivian held onto Reona's fur until
the earthquake subsided. These heroics led Ken-L Ration
to name Reona its 1989 "Dog Hero of the Year."

Stella

What she did: When Chris Georgiou fell into a 15-foot-
deep pond in Adelaide, Australia, he didn't know what to
do. Georgiou couldn't swim, and his heavy winter clothing
was making him sink fast. He called for help, but the area
around his ranch was unpopulated and no one heard his
screams . . . no people, that is. His Rottweiler, Stella, and

Border collie, Ziggy, came right away. While Ziggy barked for help, Stella jumped into the pond and swam over to her owner. Georgiou grabbed onto her and Stella pulled him to the safety of shallow water.

Weela

What she did: The Watkins family of Southern California's Imperial County found Weela, a four-week-old pit bull, in an alley. They brought her home, and she grew up alongside Gary, the family's young son. When Gary was 11, Weela dashed at him from across the yard. She knocked into the boy so hard that he fell over, and his mother jumped to her feet, startled. Weela had never attacked any of them before. When Lori Watkins reached her son and dog, she discovered that Weela was fighting a rattlesnake right where Gary had been playing. The snake bit Weela, but the dog survived—a good thing, because a few years later, she proved her heroism again. In 1993, when a nearby river overflowed during a rainstorm, Weela and Lori Watkins went looking for neighbors who needed help. As the flood-water rose, they came upon a group of stranded dogs and cats. Weela swam across the river, lugging food to the animals until they could be saved. She also led rescuers to a group of horses stranded on a manure pile and guided 30 people through shallow water to safety. For her efforts, Ken-L Ration named the pit bull its 1993 "Dog Hero of the Year."

Dixie

What she did: When a cottonmouth snake attacked young Frank, Katie, and Codi Humphries in their back-yard, Dixie, their 16-month-old pit bull, came to the res-cue. She jumped between the snake and the children and took two bites to the face before the kids' mother, Valerie, killed the snake with an axe. Dixie was unconscious and had to be rushed to the vet, where she spent several days hooked up to an antibiotic IV. Dixie eventually recovered, and her vet nominated her for the Georgia Veterinary Medical Association's "Hero Dog" award. After beating out 300 other nominees, Dixie won and was inducted into Georgia's Animal Hall of Fame.

To read about more good dogs, turn to page 6.

A Doggone Crossword

The entries here include two famous stories featuring canines and one best-selling children's book. We think you can finish this puzzle in about arf an hour. (Answers on page 227.)

ACROSS

1. Impudence—or pie "cover"
6. Snidely look
10. Smooth-talking
14. Iranian faith
15. Spanish stewpot
16. Election losers
17. 100 smackers
18. Wide-eyed sort
19. Tiny jumper
20. Sherlock Holmes uses a dog named Toby in this story
23. English actress Diana
24. Wedding cake feature
25. Corp. bigwigs
28. Okinawa's capital and chief port
30. Plays well with others
34. Beverly Sills song
36. Director Ephron
38. Dickens character Heep
39. Bestselling children's book by Janette Sebring Lowrey, with "The"
42. "With this ring ___ wed"
43. Housecat's perch
44. Moon walker Armstrong
45. Prescribed amount
47. Normandy town
49. Give it a go
50. "Eewww!"
52. Posterior
54. Richard Adams novel featuring Rowf and Snitter
59. Debts
60. Composer Khachaturian
61. Hole ___ (duffer's dream)
63. First in a set
64. Metrical foot
65. Observant one
66. Tom Cruise or Betelgeuse
67. Hgwys. on a map
68. Early anesthetic

DOWN

1. Canadian media inits.
2. Carry on
3. "Oops!"
4. Full
5. Attaches, as a rope
6. They're not likely to win
7. Verve
8. *Cats* poet

9. Palm fiber
10. Take a jog
11. "Little" girl of comics
12. Roman road
13. "Be Prepared" org.
21. Tehran resident
22. Disgusted
25. Bland; insipid
26. Combining form meaning "first"
27. Punjab sect members
29. Ars gratia ___
31. Tiny lab tube
32. Piglike animal
33. In a bashful or timid manner
35. Reply to a ship's captain
37. Physically awkward, especially with the hands
40. Boost
41. Miss ___ of *Dallas*
46. Cream puff
48. 1939 Giraudoux play
51. Gold standard
53. Start of a prohibition
54. Tugboat sound
55. Way to sway
56. Plucky
57. Teen in black, often
58. Blade in *The Mikado*
59. E.R. hookups
62. Make a mistake

Sniff It Out

We left out "mutt" and "junkyard dog," but you can still find 40 MBFs (man's best friends) in this image. Happy hunting!

AIREDALE
ALSATIAN
BASSET HOUND
BEAGLE
BEARDIE
BEDLINGTON
BIRD DOG
BOARHOUND
BORZOI
BOXER
BULLDOG
CAIRN TERRIER
CHIHUAHUA
CHOW
COCKER SPANIEL
COLLIE
CORGI
DACHSHUND
DINGO
DOBERMAN

GREAT DANE
GREYHOUND
GRIFFON
HUSKY
IRISH SETTER
KEESHOND
LABRADOR
LURCHER
MALTESE
MASTIFF
PAPILLON
PEKINGESE
POINTER
POMERANIAN
POODLE
SAINT BERNARD
SALUKI
SCHNAUZER
SHEEPDOG
WHIPPET

```
                                              K
                                            X B
                                          X P Z
                                        W C K S
                                      O P T S B
                                      L S H I E
                                    C B E R L N
                                    O E D J O A
                                  X P D Y L S M
                  F R Y X E E E D O L L A G R
                S L D R L S R O G Q I I K R E O
              T Y U B C E T G V F P N W D D B T
M L Y J G Y L C M Q Y G A T T A A T G X N C O H
N X T E K E E S H O N D G I T P B B T U I E D D
Q E Q S N Y W L E I N A P S R E K C O C L N N A
Y I U L S A L U K I H A E O R N S H N A U U U Z
  H S R F J A E L M S U N N M H T H D H O R O G
    H S B P B S C H N A U Z E R E S H W H H N
              W R D H S Z R H R I L X Y E
              D N T S U I C A G R R U E J
            T O Q C A E A A O R N O I I R X M
          P E E G L B E I D B I Z D I D E G C C
        R J P O I N T E R L T F R A R R A L R A H Y
      R K P T R O I C A G L F A R Z A O I N L K O E
    S L I     D I G R O C B S E I C B P T U W D R
  H W H       Q L L N C A M B L J Q I E F J B H Q
    W         E S E T L A M F M A S T I F F F Y F X
              L C K I T Z L V Z Y R K I W L Y W D I
```

For answers, turn to page 227.

223

Answers

Hollywood Hounds, page 21

1. **A.** The charming and sophisticated pup who played Asta was named Skippy, and he went on to star in films such as *Bringing Up Baby* and *The Awful Truth*.

2. **C.** Hooch's real name was Beasley. He was a rare breed—a dogue de Bourdeaux—who made only the 1989 film *Turner and Hooch*.

3. **C.** The dog who played Buddy also played Comet on the 1990s television series *Full House*.

4. **C.** Beethoven appeared in several theatrical sequels following the first film, and an animated TV series ran from 1994 to 1995.

5. **A.** The character of Lassie has starred in numerous radio shows, movies, television shows, and books. She was based on a character created by author Eric Knight and first appeared in a short story published in *The Saturday Evening Post* in 1938; a novel followed in 1940.

6. **A.** Discovered in an animal shelter by famous trainer Frank Inn, Benji's real name was Higgins. In the mid-1960s, before becoming a famous mutt, he had a role in the TV show *Petticoat Junction*.

7. **C.** Enzo played Skip in the film, but he was best known as one of the dogs who played Eddie on the television show *Fraiser*.

It's a Howl, page 73

1. **F.** The title of Led Zeppelin's "Black Dog" is a tribute to a nameless black pooch who loitered around England's Headley Grange recording studio during the band's recording sessions.
2. **E.** Johnny Cash got his first royalty check on March 22, 1955, for the song "Cry, Cry, Cry." The amount of the check: $2.41.
3. **A.** The popular "Hound Dog" was first recorded in 1952 by blues legend Big Mama Thornton. Big Mama was the daughter of a Baptist minister, and she ran away when she was just 14 to pursue a career in secular music. But it was Elvis Presley who made the song world-famous.
4. **G.** Although born in London, singer Nellie McKay grew up mostly in New York, and after dropping out of the Manhattan School of Music, she worked as a stand-up comic before returning to music.
5. **J.** George Michael wrote "Careless Whisper"—one of the most-played radio songs of the 1980s—when he was just 17.
6. **C.** Chris Cornell of Soundgarden and ex-members of the band Mother Love Bone formed Temple of the Dog in 1990. The men took their new band's name from a

Mother Love Bone lyric in the song "Man of Golden Words."

7. **I.** Weird Al, who's made a living doing parodies of popular songs, learned to play the accordion (his signature instrument) when he was seven years old.

8. **B.** George Clinton has earned many nicknames over the years, including "the Prime Minister of Funk" and "the King of Interplanetary Funksmanship."

9. **H.** Mega rap star Snoop Dogg got his stage name as a child when his mother nicknamed him "Snoopy" because he loved the *Peanuts* cartoon character.

10. **D.** Grammy Award winner Patti Page was born Clara Ann Fowler in 1927. She changed her name in the 1940s when she started singing on a radio show sponsored by the Page Milk Company.

Fine Art Fidos, page 98

1. *Dogs Playing Poker*
2. Andy Warhol
3. Henri Toulouse-Lautrec
4. *The Garden of Earthly Delights*
5. Pablo Picasso
6. Frida Kahlo
7. Jean-Michel Basquiat
8. Fidelity

Paws on the Page, page 157

1. Jack
2. Luath and Bodger
3. Fang
4. Bull's Eye
5. Toto
6. Prince Terrian
7. Nana
8. Buck
9. Patrasche
10. Boots

First Friends, page 215

1. A 2. C 3. B 4. C 5. A 6. B

A Doggone Crossword, page 220

C	R	U	S	T		L	E	E	R		G	L	I	B
B	A	H	A	I		O	L	L	A		O	U	T	S
C	N	O	T	E		N	A	I	F		F	L	E	A
	T	H	E	S	I	G	N	O	F	F	O	U	R	
		D	O	R	S		T	I	E	R				
V	P	S		N	A	H	A		A	D	A	P	T	S
A	R	I	A		N	O	R	A		U	R	I	A	H
P	O	K	Y	L	I	T	T	L	E	P	U	P	P	Y
I	T	H	E	E		S	I	L	L		N	E	I	L
D	O	S	A	G	E		S	T	L	O		T	R	Y
		Y	U	C	K		H	I	N	D				
	T	H	E	P	L	A	G	U	E	D	O	G	S	
I	O	U	S		A	R	A	M		I	N	O	N	E
V	O	L	I		I	A	M	B		N	O	T	E	R
S	T	A	R		R	T	E	S		E	T	H	E	R

Sniff It Out, page 222

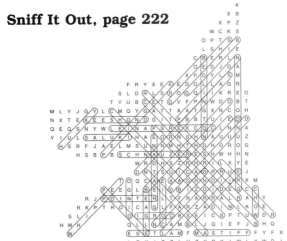

The Last Page

Sit down and be counted!
Become a member of the Bathroom Readers'
Institute! No join-up fees, monthly minimums or maxi-
mums, organized dance parties, quilting bees, solicitors,
annoying phone calls (we only have one phone line),
spam—or any other canned meat product—to worry about
. . . just the chance to get our fabulous monthly newsletter
and (if you want) some extremely cool Uncle John's stuff.

So check our Web site:
www.bathroomreader.com

Or send us a letter:
Uncle John's Bathroom Reader
Portable Press
10350 Barnes Canyon Road
San Diego, CA 92121

Or email us at unclejohn@btol.com.

Hope you enjoyed the book—and if you're skipping to the
end, what are you doing reading this page? Go back and
finish!